Suspicious History

Suspicious History

Questioning the Basis of Historical Evidence

Jack Zevin

ROWMAN & LITTLEFIELD PUBLISHERS
Lanham • Boulder • New York • London

Published by Rowman & Littlefield
An imprint of The Rowman & Littlefield Publishing Group, Inc.
4501 Forbes Boulevard, Suite 200, Lanham, Maryland 20706
www.rowman.com

6 Tinworth Street, London SE11 5AL, United Kingdom

Copyright © 2021 by Jack Zevin

All rights reserved. No part of this book may be reproduced in any form or by any electronic or mechanical means, including information storage and retrieval systems, without written permission from the publisher, except by a reviewer who may quote passages in a review.

British Library Cataloguing in Publication Information Available

Library of Congress Cataloging-in-Publication Data

Names: Zevin, Jack, author.
Title: Suspicious history : questioning the bases of historical evidence / Jack Zevin.
Description: Lanham : Rowman & Littlefield, [2021] | Includes bibliographical references and index.
Identifiers: LCCN 2020049953 (print) | LCCN 2020049954 (ebook) |
  ISBN 9781475853162 (cloth) | ISBN 9781475853179 (paperback) |
  ISBN 9781475853186 (epub)
Subjects: LCSH: History—Study and teaching. | Social sciences—Study and teaching.
Classification: LCC D16.2 .Z48 2021 (print) | LCC D16.2 (ebook) | DDC 907.1—dc23
LC record available at https://lccn.loc.gov/2020049953
LC ebook record available at https://lccn.loc.gov/2020049954

Contents

Introduction   1

1   Suspicious!: Alerting Ourselves to the Suspicions, Dangers, and Excitements of Historical Thinking   7

2   Facts: Data as Information, Evidence, Stuff, Content, and So On   27

3   Bias: Human Prejudice and Feelings of Superiority   55

4   Story: Fact and Fiction and in Between   79

5   Lenses: Multiple Perspectives in the Teaching and Learning of History   103

6   Pedestal: Idolizing and Glorifying versus Demonizing and Deprecating ((Super)heroines and (Super)heroes, and Real Villains and Villainesses)   131

Index   165

About the Author   169

Introduction

The Master said, "A true teacher is one who, keeping the past alive, is also able to understand the present." (Analects 2.11)

—Confucius

The study of history should be a mind-altering encounter that leaves one forever unable to consider the social world without asking questions about where a claim comes from, who's making it, and how time and place shape human behavior.

—Sam Wineburg

HEADLINE!

Stanford researchers find student have trouble judging the credibility of information online. www.stanford.edu/wineburg/. November 22, 2016.[1]

INTRODUCTION: MY LIFE IN THE HISTORY AND SOCIAL STUDIES CLASSROOM, THEN AND NOW

When I started out in the social studies profession as a high school history teacher in Chicago in the 1960s, I was an ardent fan of curriculum reform in the direction of more debate, discussion, and inquiry. Most of my colleagues and I especially wanted to get away from the standard, boring, and mostly didactic lessons of the time that assumed "truth" in textbooks.[2] We wanted to escape the entirely predictable "legacy" curriculum of "we're the greatest" and "how a bill becomes a law." We hoped for "open discussion" and argument, not polite silence taking notes.

Social studies teachers wanted to share the original stuff of history, the documentary evidence that texts were based on, a foundation of primary sources. This meant teaching kids (and teachers and parents) how to do the "new" social studies of that period in history, the 1960s and 1970s, how to conduct an inquiry, to really read a text like an historian or social scientists.[3] Our experiment wished not to just walk away with the seeming facts, the whole facts, and nothing but the altogether true facts. The hope was that every teacher would be a professional interested in teaching the habits of mind of historians and social scientists.

Social studies would be transformed from textbook canned lessons into direct contact with primary or original sources. Documentary evidence was the end all and be all basis for inquiry. Secondary sources, the work of professionals, were welcome but only if students had a basis for grasping the story and recognizing at least partially what the historian's work was based upon, and how the interpreter had handled the originals to form a story.[4]

A movement had sprung up in the 1960s and 1970s called "The New Social Studies," largely forgotten now by those who abandon history (which includes most, even professional educators).[5] Many also lack curiosity to research where ideas are coming from, and ask if the past is anything different than the present. Even among many historians and social studies professionals there appears to be considerable memory loss on the origins of intense efforts to fundamentally change the way history and social science are taught at all school levels.

Yet the ideas of the movement are often adhered to still by the aging innovators, and many new recruits, although relabeled and rediscovered by new representatives to our fields of inquiry every decade or so.[6] In fact, the National Council for the Social Studies has recently promulgated a new set of standards, the C3 Framework (2015) that establishes as doctrine an "arc of inquiry."[7] This is, in my view, not substantially different than what we did in the 1960s and arguably less creative.

Any single set of C3 goals is probably enough to keep a class busy for a year or more, and demands a level of thinking most of us would be happy to see achieved in college courses.

This process of institutionalization took about fifty years or so, and has come at a time in the 2010s and 2020s when, ironically, a conservative, rather anti-scientific government is now in charge of the United States, including, of course, the minor subject of education, and the even more minor fields of history and social studies.

The vast majority of social studies teachers and historian professionals at least give lip service to inquiry and problem solving, as deeply held goals they subscribe to for the nation and their own classrooms. Many are strong advocates of teaching critical thinking and following the arc of inquiry to learner conclusions and insights. But in the present day we are also inundated with digital data that may mislead as well as inform.[8]

Over the decades, we have added whole new waves of vocabulary and "edspeak" to the way we converse about history and social studies goals that include critical thinking, discovery, higher-order learning and thinking, thinking like an historian, inferential reasoning, self-guided learning, and problem solving. A heavy load to say the least!

After decades of adding new approaches, changing the curriculum, rediscovering the wheel, and re-researching effects, we have come yet again to the profound conclusion that students learn history best (meaning most deeply, and insightfully) when they struggle with big questions connected to the primary and secondary sources.[9] Presenting history and the social sciences in all their messy and confusing detail invites serious detective work and argument. Habits of mind have returned.

However, after working as a teacher, curriculum writer, professor, and consultant, I must say that while the academic professionals pretty much agree on inquiry goals, the schools still suffer from the same problems as the ones I started teaching in fifty years ago. And the bottom line is still "facts," knowing rather than thinking, and not thinking too critically at that, especially about our own nation's story!

After all, with a lot of "critical thinking," you might get in trouble if you arouse too much controversy and, worse yet, question the shibboleths, sacred cow texts, of U.S. history! World texts, ancient texts, you can pretty much kick around except for some worshipping of the Athenian Democracy, the Roman Republic, and John Locke, forgiving him being British.

There is now widespread acceptance of historical habits of mind and critical thinking among social studies professionals, but there is little evidence to prove that the instructional field as a whole agrees and practices history, civics, and economics as subjects of inquiry.

Many teachers still like to tell stories and persist in giving "answers" that abnegate scholarly and thoughtful goals for the profession. Many teachers avoid controversial issues or even mild controversy, and many don't know their history or social science in more than a cursory textbookish kind of way.

Since we do not have comprehensive studies or national random samples of social studies/history teachers and students, with the exception of every few years, we are sort of shooting in the dark for these conclusions. But there are decades of smaller studies that would indicate and argue that the field has hardly been swept over by an epidemic of open-mindedness and critical thinking.

Larry Cuban, among others, argues that over many decades we are pretty much running in place on teaching historical habits of mind, with a few exceptions.[10]

So, I am proposing to share a book with you about teaching history in ways that purposely and specifically gets us into trouble by filling our curriculum with higher-order questions, conflicting interpretations, critical reviews, confusing narratives, disagreeable sources, and ethical issues inviting judgments.

So, we need to begin by un-privileging U.S. history, *viewing all history* as that of the Sapiens species, a species that has a mixed and evolving background, messy habits of mind, and has been conditioned by a vast array of cultures and causes to avoid truth in history as a name brand.

To shake things up, including ourselves, take a global view of history going back to the stone age, and spend a minimum of a measly quarter time more on women, gender, racial and ethnic groups, and the lower social classes. Pay a quarter time less to men, conquests, commerce, and warfare, and avoid people dressed in wigs and breeches.

Let's join in a commitment to illuminate and understand the baggage of history, a history that never goes away, even when we are unaware of it. So, let's build awareness of others by relating past to present, and present to past, and past and present to imminent futures. Look at history through other lenses, stand in others' shoes, and jump into arguments about who is wonderful or wicked.

Violate all the rules by questioning facts and by formulating chancy prescriptions and questionable predictions. Join together in adopting a view of evidence and interpretations that says, *be suspicious*! Work on neutralizing our culturally conditioned ethnocentrism and egotism. Think more like an anthropologist living with other cultures. Consider "us" as much as people as "them."

Focus on teaching mainly problem-inducing tough, stringy, meaty parts, with some raw veggies tossed in, and skip the unctuous gravy of edited content, unsupported claims, and ethnocentrism, as well as lending credence to uncorroborated tweets, fake news, and unchecked self-serving nationalistic narratives.

Suspicious! will be laid out across two volumes, each raising questions about truth and trustworthiness in history and social studies. This, the first volume, will focus mainly on questions of factual evidence as distorted through biases, storytelling, multiple viewpoints (lenses), and the very human desire to promote and honor, or ignore, demote, and dishonor people, places, and events in the story of humankind. Teaching "real" history with all the warts on gives you the opportunity to look at accounts and reports from past and present in new and perhaps provocative ways.

You can open each chapter of this book with challenges provoked by questions focused on one or more of the following five themes:

1. Facts/evidence
2. Bias
3. Story
4. Lenses
5. Pedestals

Feel free throughout to add themes and topics of your own to generate new questions. Keep in mind that volume 2 will feature related themes including "fakes" restorations, interpretations, controversy, rules, and wickedness.

History and social science have always been about understanding human behavior, and ourselves. And Sapiens still has pretty much the same problems telling an accurate and unemotional story probably dating back to the Stone Age. We are self-centered, "all about us" selfie photographers. New lenses and less bias would go a long way to correct the mistakes of history and create new and more uniting stories than we have nowadays.

Help make your school and community sensitive in ways that push us to view the world as a single planet divided into many large and small properties that we call states, nations, and empires. Consider the globe as a single united entity facing its greatest challenge in history: environmental change and destruction.

Remember we are "smart" mammals living in a biome right along with everyone else! But we don't seem to be responding to new historical challenges of climate change and information overload.

So, take a challenge, try to step into a history and a social science that offers the same privileges to all. Excuse no one from examining their place on a pedestal or cast into the margins of history (though we need always to explain the meaning of our terms) and open the door to multiple interpretations of people, places, policies, and events in and out of classrooms.

NOTES

1. McGrew, S., Smith, M., Breakstone, J., Ortega, T., & Wineburg, S. (2019). Improving university students' web savvy: An intervention study. *The British Journal of Educational Psychology.*

2. Massialas, B. G., and Zevin, J. (1967). *Creative Encounters in the Classroom*. New York: John Wiley and Sons.

3. Cuban, L. (2016). *Teaching History Then and Now: A Story of Stability and Change in Schools*. Cambridge, MA: Harvard Education Press.

4. Cuban, L. (1984) How Teachers Taught: Constancy and Change in American Classrooms, 1890–1980. Research on Teaching Monograph Series, 1st Ed.

5. Wineburg, S. (2001). *Historical Thinking and Other Unnatural Acts: Changing the Future of Teaching the Past*. Philadelphia: Temple University Press.

6. Martin, D. S., and Wineburg, S. S. (2008). "Seeing thinking on the web" *The History Teacher* 41(3), 305–319.

7. Swan, K. Project Director and Lead Writer (2010). *College Career, and Civic Life, C3 Framework*. Silver Spring, MD: National Council for the Social Studies.

8. High-Tech Schools and Low-Tech Teaching. A Commentary. L Cuban—*Journal of Computing in Teacher Education*, 1998—ERIC.

9. Breakstone, J., McGrew, Smith, S., Ortega, T., and Wineburg, S. (2018) "Why we need a new approach to teaching digital literacy" *Phi Delta Kappan* 99(6), 27–32.

10. Wilson, S. M., and Wineburg, S. S. (2014). "Peering at history through different lenses: The role of disciplinary perspectives in teaching history" *Teachers College Record* 89(4), 525–539.

Chapter 1

Suspicious!

Alerting Ourselves to the Suspicions, Dangers, and Excitements of Historical Thinking

The best reason to learn history: not in order to predict the future, but to free yourself of the past and imagine alternative destinies. Of course, this is not total freedom—we cannot avoid being shaped by the past. But some freedom is better than none.

—Yuval Noah Harari, *Homo Deus: A Brief History of Tomorrow* (2018)

"Suspicious: causing one to have the idea or impression that something or someone is of questionable, dishonest, or dangerous character or condition. Doubtful, dubious, unsure, wary, skeptical."[1]

Does this definition seem adequate in describing the feeling of discomfort in facing potential fake news, lies, and corruption in historical and social science accounts?

OVERVIEW

This chapter raises questions about precisely what constitutes exciting and critical teaching of history and social science. What is true, false, and in-between become topics of discussion and debate.

> **HEADLINE: CHECK IT OUT!**
>
> Even if you could get people tools to distinguish truth from fiction, would people care enough to use those tools? The information Society Project/Floyd Abrams Institute for Freedom of Expression. www.law.yale.edu

I. INTRODUCTION

History is among the most dangerous subjects taught. We should maintain an active sense of suspicion about origins, sources, and authors.

Historical and social science narratives and analyses are prone to a wide range of infections and inflections, views and reviews, some patently false, some virtually truth-resistant, and others reasonably accurate. To separate the fake from the factual is not an easy task, one that is becoming more difficult in daily life.

But this is exactly our opportunity as teachers and students to enliven inquiry, to shake up regular patterns of instruction, and to introduce new perspectives on history.[2]

Modern technology, particularly the handy-dandy, all-purpose, current obsession of local, national, and global citizens, the cell phone is the major purveyor of information for individuals. The phone is followed, expanded, and supplemented by larger devices ranging from iPads to computers to movie screens.[3]

Technology of this kind may be called the "net" stream, information that is delivered to cell phone/computer/tablet. However, the same authors are all purveying pretty much the same information from the same or similar sources: some correctly identified, others not so, or not identified at all.

Authorship and origin are not always clear. Worse yet, news, data, and the information being conveyed to us is often by third parties or shadow sources, representing distinct points of view and biases. But users seldom ask for or check points of origin expressing trust for the communicated word and image.[4]

Suspicion of sources, corroborating sources, and determining sources are a major part of history, the social sciences, and social studies education.[5] Yet more and more students and teachers go with the flow of electronic data, and rarely raise issues about editing, management, fake news, and sins of omission and commission. As emails expand to fill the allotted space and time, less and less attention is directed to sources or to content.[6] Process reigns supreme, but the cost is a loss of sense of veracity, of struggle with message and meaning, and of historical context.

This book aims to help teachers and learners treat content as important, open to multiple interpretations, and capable of inspiring positive, neutral, and negative feelings about human behavior in the evolution of history. As a species, we have special abilities and problems that need to be kept in mind in making sense of past, present, and potential future.

II. ASSERTIONS ABOUT HISTORY

- Never before in human history has so much information been so readily available at so cheap a price.[7]
- Never before in human history has the horizon of history shrunk so much into the present.
- Never before in human history has there been so great a degree of unawareness of the past as we drag the baggage of culture, society, and time with us into the "now."
- Never before in human history has the common person been so able to access so many "facts" in zip time.
- Never before has communication for the common person been so instant, so easy, so widespread, so absorbing, and yet so banal.
- Never before in human history are we so accepting of multitudinous sources, often conflicting, all offered as factual and verified.
- Never before have we, the global users of the Internet known so much about daily drivel and so little about context, viewpoints, or the lifestyles of "others" around the globe.
- Never before have we been so easily distracted by current events that obscure the meaning of the past.
- Never before have we allowed ourselves so little time for boredom, so little time for reflection into deeper meaning for ourselves and for human history.

Thus, I will argue that we are at a crisis point in the way history is taught, and learned, as conveyed through media. The teaching and learning of history are mostly still locked into a paper and pencil past dependent on historians and social scientists competing with the deluge of news and views, most of it based on dot-com traffic. Information, too, is edited, structured, and managed so we are not always sure of its authenticity.

Even the structure (topics, outlines, format) of courses at all levels are shaped by a largely narrative tradition that reflects national entities, not global concerns.

Information is at our fingertips, courtesy of the world wide web, with multitudinous websites where we can find "anything" we want. Of course, there are a few problems, for example, sourcing, contextualization, and corroboration. And this before we even get to hard parts: disagreement, conflicting views, multiple interpretations, and ethical challenges like fake news.

Clouds of data hover over us, and we are frequently warned about "backing up" our data, photos, music, and secret Swiss bank accounts to the iCloud.

Companies are making money off the cloud, and more and more documents are digitized. And more surprising, we feel quite safe about it and most of us do what is directed with little or no doubt resulting in gobzillions of data placed in storage. We should really be trading in bitcoins of history, testing which leaders, economies, and societies go up and which go down in value.

In order to dig out and make sense of history, now and then, and relationships between subjects, we need to know which questions to ask of the milky way of data. If we have never heard of Mother Jones from Chicago, then we can find out about her and realize that an important first-rate woman of accomplishment has passed our way in history. She is somebody we might be willing to pay as much attention to her in the classroom as a third-rate white male president.

Do we have a sense of history about what is stored away? Do we look back or always look to the present to collect more electronic stuffing? Do we know how to handle and interpret the messages, photos, music, videos, and other data we have stored? Though electronic, and so easy to collect, all of the data still suffers from the eons-old vicissitudes of historical and social science thinking.[8] Yes, we are very "advanced" but still suffer from the same sociological (race and gender), political (power and privilege), and historical (time and space) defects that were part of the first stirrings of civilizations around seven thousand years ago.[9]

Our journey has been remarkably brief and rapid, with powerful consequences, and we gather more gobs of data while the effects of climate change charges upon us.

a. Suspicions Listed

Perhaps we can make a list of the "suspicions" of teaching and learning history and the social sciences, and social studies, clearer: The layout of this book begins with an introduction to the teaching and learning of history and the social sciences then proceeds to investigate how history/social sciences can be presented in an AGE of fake news, and conflicting accounts, to stimulate thinking about key problems in acquiring knowledge and understanding, and making decisions about what and whom to believe.

These problems are divided into eight chapters beginning with "facts," bias, story, and interpretation to pedestal, lenses, and wickedness. Each chapter delves into issues and difficult problems inherent in the social sciences and history that, rather than be avoided, can create great excitement with an impetus to become skillful detectives of past, present, and maybe predicting futures. Finally, the book ends with a wrap-up of major issues and *a plea for changing teaching styles* from storytelling, and data collection, to reflective, critical, and downright annoying commitment to thinking and being *suspicious!*

1. *Suspicious! The "facts," the evidence, and the data*
   We need to check the documents and websites for authorship, time, place, and veracity. In other words, *is the source authentic*: of the time and place it purports, or if later then researched by a professional historian or social scientist? Are there other sources we would like to have: is literature an option?
2. *Suspicious! Awareness of bias/hidden agenda/prejudice*
   We need to critically examine each of the documents and websites to find out if they have an agenda, hidden or public: Are there biases, attitudes, and ideologies the writers and designers want to get across to people?
3. *Suspicious! Story and History/narrative styles; plot, characters, motives, morals*
   We need to recognize the author's style and purpose, how plots and characters evolve, and where symbols and signs are important, as well as distinguish fact from fiction, or merge literature with history?
4. *Suspicious! Interpretation/Explanation/Hypothesis*
   We need to recognize when interpretations (not just facts) are offered, and when explanations are given; and to what degree are these based (or not) on the historical evidence available, or perhaps literary inventions?
5. *Suspicious! Pedestal, Heroines and Heroes in History*
   We need to coolly review and probe who and why some people, and some categories of people, are placed on a social, political, or cultural pedestal while others are left out entirely or marginalized in history, the representation of gender, race, and class status.
6. *Suspicious! Lenses/Viewpoints/Perspectives*
   We need to sharpen sensitivity to the wearing of different lenses, of different colors, shapes, and foci that people use to generate varying perspectives about people, places, and events throughout past and present.
7. *Suspicious! Wickedness/Morals/Ethics/Judgments*
   We need to inquire into our own feelings and those of our students to find an ethical and moral dimension in history and render some sort of judgment, however inadequate. Are there issues and feelings we would like to share and debate openly?

III. AGE-OLD PROBLEMS

To deal with these age-old, investigative human problems, intensive historical training and habits of thinking are the perfect vehicles to engage the challenges of an information age in the twenty-first century and beyond.[10] Much greater tsunamis of news and views will soon overtake us.

Assuming you and yours can be convinced to adopt quite a different set of approaches that cast a critical mind to the teaching of history is the hope of this book. And this is assuming we can go back to the days of patient and boring investigations of documentary evidence, pondering meaning and arguing methods. In effect, we need to teach "deep thinking" about historical evidence whether a thousand years or a minute old. But we are also ready to employ new and innovative digital techniques to analyze the vast and increasing quantities of knowledge coming our way, arranged for us by website after website.

In almost every history and social studies classroom, the bottom line is "which facts students need to know," usually embedded in a story that is already an interpretation, with feelings added. This interpretation may be both conscious and unconscious, in the sense that the conscious part is seeking to influence readers to adopt a specific agenda.

The unconscious part has assumed certain evidence to be open to manipulation, so it comes out sounding better put together than is warranted by close examination of sources.[11] Real sources can be quite messy and provoke a bounty of questions, and that is exactly what we wish for to make teaching and learning exciting.

Deeply embedded in history instruction at all levels are assumptions that we are engaged in a scientific enterprise of fact collection, comparison, and critical analysis. We are working at drawing solid conclusions. But we are also engaged in an artistic endeavor of literary reconstruction and invention, with a distinct cast of characters, plus a sense of building a judgmental framework to assign ratings: love or hate to events and figures from the past.[12]

The enterprise of teaching and understanding history includes the following list of built-in conflicts:

a. Teaching traditions: tending toward storyteller versus the questioner
b. The structure of history: write big or writ small or in-between?
c. The bottom line is: questions or answers
d. The curriculum: boring and deadly, but neat, or exciting, messy and annoying?
e. The goals: factual conclusions over conflicting evidence, or vice versa?
f. The problems: ambiguity and dilemma, or clarity and certainty?

IV. ENTERING THE DIGITAL AGE OF OVERWHELMING RESOURCES

Sowing the seeds of doubt, and sharing the "mess," is a method among us that helps make us sensitive to understanding the past, as opposed to professionals connecting the dots and resolving the issues for ourselves and others! Solving the problems and handing out labels is too easy to be truthful.

So, let's set up our own *No. 1 Ladies and Gentlemen's Detective Agency for Incontrovertible Evidence and Theory*, to investigate history. Let's cultivate a sense of history with all the warts on, all the issues staring us in the face, all the complexities and confusion that reflect real life and the nature of evidence. Let us revive the notion of becoming historical detectives aware of and delighted in the dangers that confront us. Use more visuals to connect past to present.[13]

And let us *not* accept single right answers ever, especially from the Internet! Rather let us fear right answers as already formulated conclusions and opinions that we should have made on our own, or at least questioned. And let us permit ourselves to develop and share feelings about the past, but avoid dogmatic judgments that lock us into one attitude or feeling over all others.

In other words, keep the mind open and allow yourself to enter doubt, keeping an eye open for new evidence and new interpretation, all the while restraining moral judgment. Detectives need to find and follow clues, and eventually draw conclusions, always leaving an open mind to new evidence. They should wait patiently before finding a moral in a case, even an extreme case.

Therefore, a quick and easy ten rules are proposed here, from beginning an investigation to its end, building upon our evidence and verifying sources:

1. Be suspicious
2. Collect evidence
3. Check sources
4. Find clues
5. Analyze stories
6. Contest views
7. Develop interpretations
8. Derive theories
9. Build proofs
10. Defend judgments

a. Key Considerations in Teaching and Learning History (Thinking like a historian/social scientist/great detective)

There are vast lists, objectives, goals, standards, requirements, habits of mind, ways of historical thinking, and instructional guides to define (and hamper) your joy and clarity of thinking in teaching history and the social sciences.

So, why don't we settle on just a few essentials that will get you into trouble in designing and implementing your lesson plans. The website www.history.org argues that there are "five core components of historical thinking" that can help us organize our investigations, that is:

1. Multiple Accounts and Perspectives
2. Analysis of Primary Documents
3. Sourcing of original content
4. Understanding Historical Context
5. Claim-Evidence Connection[14]

We can pretty much agree with this short list of "components" but I would change the order from the simpler to the more complex processes of historical thinking. Perhaps we would add a sixth dimension concerning emotion, the state of feeling, and expression of affect in historical evidence.

Sourcing should be first since it is needed before we really get around to asking more difficult questions. It should be simple, of course, who, what, where, when, but sometimes it isn't and you have to chase a source around quite a bit hoping you will find the "original." Yikes! it might be a translation, or it could be a forgery, or worse yet be taken from a website, for example, "www.anythingyouwanttoknowabouthistory.com!"

This could be fun and result in something like trying to catch gophers with a fishhook.

Claim-evidence connection is awkward, but important, and I would place this as a second step up from asking for checks on claims. Do we have any evidence that the gold mine is ours: is there proof of ownership and do we have authentic papers or records to prove ownership? In other words, how do we prove what we say or write? Evidence checks for claims holds the promise of keeping everyone busy checking facts, false news, and outright lies by reviewing everything everyone says not as facts but as "claims." Claims has a nice rather nineteenth-century gold rush feel to it, and also raises questions about "claim jumpers" and fool's gold.

Analysis of primary sources is a vital historical step toward making sense of the contents of primary sources. Primary sources are indeed the basis for building claims, creating interpretations, and drawing inferences about historical cause and effect. A document, image, or sound does not in itself tell you what it means: that takes work and detailed combing of the evidence for clues, leading to understanding, and conclusions (supported by evidence).

Analysis has a nice weighty feel to it like we are sharing sources with a chemist or psychiatrist who will give us insight into motivation, message, and meaning, and the pursuit of "truth." We might even be able to develop a formula to interpret the content!

Multiple accounts and perspectives lead us to the all-important concept of corroboration and questions of reliability and validity. How do we know witnesses are telling the truth, and how do we establish rules for the admission of evidence into classroom and courtroom. Even shopping sales raises questions: are the prices too good to be true, if so, be suspicious.

What if there is only one eyewitness, or two that contradict each other, or three that tell nearly different stories? What if all the witnesses have an agenda, an ax to grind, a perspective that may shape, edit, and distort reporting of the historical "facts." Oh no, we have more than one view to deal with, or not enough views, or too many views.

What about having experts go over all the evidence for us, you know, historians, sociologists, and the like, and provide the answers?

The professionals will all give the same diagnosis and treatment no doubt, and we shall be saved from thinking for ourselves, hurrah! But hold on here, the historians and social scientists and archeologist differ in their views, don't agree on how to interpret the evidence, worry about missing pieces, inaccuracies, bloated claims, and willful theorizing. This is like being in a fifteen-car pileup on Route 80, and examining the police reports to find out who caused the crash: result, no fault insurance.

Understanding historical context is a rather sophisticated concept implying that one can grasp "context" often blithely listed in teaching and learning goals easily getting a grip on a time or place by reading one or two sources or even an entire book on the subject.[15] A lot depends on what you mean by understanding, of course, and that leads to questions of depth and breadth not easily solved in an average history classroom.

Grasping life once lived in a past time and place requires a considerable quantity and quality of sources, checked for claims against evidence.[16] Data should be built upon a foundation of comprehended and comprehensible primary sources that yield inferences about habits, economics, social classes, art, music and literature, government, and sports. Visuals should be used as often as possible to help students develop a sense of identity for others and to assist in building a strong sense of context.[17]

Insight into and interpretations or generalizations about context thus require many preceding steps to rise to the top of the thinking pyramid. It is like an imagined procession behind the king and high priest as they ascend the impressively steep steps on a Central American Pyramid somewhere in the Yucatan around 500 ACE to make a sacrifice to the Gods. You get a clearer view each step up but a bit more tired and worried about what's on top or can you come down. Worse yet, you probably have to keep singing along the way to the Temple at the Top where the human sacrifices take place.

Expressing historical feelings is always there no matter how many claims are made for objectivity and truth. In fact, the more claims made the more suspicious you should become. Since history is about human activity and we are all always engaged in activities that involve power plays, affection, hatred, glory, and rebellion.[18] Among the many specifically human historical activities possible, one should be on guard against being swept away by emotional conclusions. Instead, wait for a review of claim-evidence connections.

Yet it is very human to empathize or sympathize with human predicaments even if they are thousands of years back in the past or thousands of years in the future. The species seems to have some of the same built-in problems and features, like aggression, love, jealousy, ambition, and artistic expression. These qualities need to be sourced, analyzed, and connected just as other evidence is reviewed, preferably before jumping to conclusions or taking sides.

Resist establishing a sudden positive or negative stance toward people, places, and events. Tame emotions but do not deny them in history and the social sciences. Give people of past times the benefit of the doubt: they may have limited knowledge and think they are conveying truthful data. But they may also be entertaining their audience, an audience much more local and probably less educated than the author or artist.

b. Tales of Travel: Hearsay as Evidence

A major way to leap out of context is to leap into two contexts simultaneously is to encourage comparisons between past and present people, places, and events. Even if this is not perfect it shows historical continuity, and invites a challenge for you and your students to decide if comparisons are fair and analogies workable. Relating past to present, present to past, also offers a justification for learning and teaching history, showing that (within limits and particulars) human beings have persisting issues to consider, and perennial problems of society and politics, economics and culture, to work out.

Circumstances create effects and adaptations that may be repeated from age to age, or may appear in many ages. There are always questions of uniqueness and analogy, but examining evidence helps move an historical discussion forward, providing students with comparison and contrast strategies to work out. Teachers can also challenge students to expand the context to other nations and cultures, or to move across time zones.

Societies can be examined for likeness and difference that may be very valuable in understanding the present as prelude to the future. This is not idle speculation, but reflection on the pressures, developments, and shifts of our own time. What is an acceptable story in one society may be wholly laughable in another! But beware of smugness because the flow of claims and counterclaims in fake news alerts can spring up in our own news flows and blogs.

The present is an outgrowth of many pasts. We are all dragging the entire history of the planet around with us whether we are aware of that or not. Our language, tastes, foods, sex beliefs and practices, technology, and values arrived from the past. These may be reinterpreted in the present or may remain surprisingly much as they were decades or centuries ago. The baggage is immense which is why history must be studies if each of us is to achieve at least a modest understanding of the world around us and our roles in it.

In the spirit of inquiry, let us remain suspicious, but open minded, with regard to understanding the context of globe, nation, and locality, and checking suggestions that are made to solve our problems, especially easy-sounding solutions.

c. Sample the Evidence: Real News or Fake?

Let's move to our jobs in the No. 1 Historical Detective Agency, find the facts, check the sources, critique the conclusions, and express our own views and emotions about what should, could, would happen next! We have discovered an interesting document, but it seems to present a lot of problems, and that is just why we want to read and examine it.

In addition, the document evokes a number of questions about historical truth, language, and the author's veracity. As a test case investigate the document below from the famous "travel" book *Mandeville's Travels* by Sir John Mandeville from the fourteenth century (circa 1322–1330). We shall also look at a few pictures that will help us develop hypotheses about what might be true and what might be false in Sir John's account.

SUSPICIOUS? SAMPLE THE EVIDENCE!

Real News or Fake?

The author claims to be an English knight who traveled widely serving with the Great Khan's military force, that is, Genghis Khan, and wrote a book about his travels across Africa, Europe, and Asia in the early to middle fourteenth century (dates not exact) and was widely read at the time and later, with illustrations added later (fourteenth, fifteenth, and eighteenth centuries) of the various peoples, plants, and places purportedly visited. It is not known for certain if Mandeville was French or English by origin, with many scholars arguing he was French, writing as an English character, for fun. Who he was and what he really believed is open to question, as is the issue of truth about the many cultures he describes, much of which was likely invented totally, but we are not always sure. It seems that many readers in medieval times read Sir John, but how much was believed is open to speculation as there were no satisfaction or fake news surveys in them those days. Legend and fantasy were often part of medieval history, and relatively few people could read that well, but there was a growing audience for travel, real and imagined.

So here is your opportunity to solve some of the mysteries of a curious and perhaps amusing book, a small portion of which (with one illustration) is presented for your reading, analysis, and critical reaction. Why might the author have composed the book, and how much of what he says in it is truthful, fantastic, or fairy tale? How can you tell? How about the language: is it personal and friendly or formal and scientific, allowing for "olde Englishe" writing forms and bad spelling?

Questions

- Where are we in the world? Can you decide?
- What are "diverse folk," according to the author? Would you like to meet them? Why or why not?
- Might there be an island people who eat raw fish? Do you?
- Could there, would there, be people with eyen in their shoulders, no heads, or have ears that hang down toward their knees? Is that possible?
- Are there dwarf people? Dwarf people who sip from pipes?
- People that move, swing, through trees? Is there confusion here: are they talking about apes of some kind perhaps? Or is this totally invented?
- Can a person be both man and woman? How? Has there ever been such people?
- Horses of 7-feet high, or folks with eight toes?
- Where are these ideas coming from? Are they based on fact or fantasy, and in what proportions, 50/50? How can an historian tell?
- And why would a travel writer like this be so appealing? Is travel still popular and can you find the truth about where you are going or does the travel agent make the trip sound better than it really could be? Why?
- Do we still like fantasy or do we prefer total truth, and how do we decide what is and what is not true?
- How about the plant that bears sheep? What do you think that was based on: truth or science fiction?
- Is this fake news or real news, in your opinion, and why?

The Travels of SIR JOHN MANDEVILLE

The king of this isle is a full great lord and a mighty, and hath under him fifty-four great isles that give tribute to him. And in everych of these isles is a king crowned; and all pay obeisance to that king. And he hath in those isles many diverse folk.

In one of these isles be folk of great stature, as giants. And they be hideous for to look upon. And they have but one eye, and that is in the middle of the front. And they eat nothing but raw flesh and raw fish. And in another isle toward the south dwell folk of foul stature and of cursed kind that have no heads. And their eyen be in their shoulders.

And in another isle be folk that have the face all flat, all plain, without nose and without mouth. But they have two small holes, all round, instead of their eyes, and their mouth is plat also without lips. And in another isle be folk of foul fashion and shape that have the lip above the mouth so great, that when they sleep in the sun they cover all the face with that lip.

And in another isle there be little folk, as dwarfs. And they be two so much as the pigmies. And they have no mouth: but instead of their mouth they have a little round hole, and when they shall eat or drink, they take through a pipe or a pen or such a thing, and suck it in, for they have no tongue; and therefore they speak not,

Figure 1.1 The Magician Joseph Dunninger with students from Columbia University demonstrating how the Indian rope trick can be performed by camera trickery. Indian rope trick faked in pictures. Life Magazine 16, June 1941, 80–81.

but they make a manner of hissing as an adder doth, and they make signs one to another as monks do, by the which every of them understandeth other.

And in another isle be folk that have great ears and long that hang down to their knees.

And in another isle be folk that have horses 7 feet. And they be strong and mighty, and swift runners; for they take wild beasts with running, and eat them.

And in another isle be folk that go upon their hands and their feet as beasts. And they be all skinned and feathered, and they will leap as lightly into trees, and from tree to tree, as it were squirrels or apes.

And in another isle be folk that be both man and woman ....

And in another isle be folk that go always upon their knees full marvelously. And at every pace that they go, it seemeth that they would fall. And they have in every foot eight toes.[19]

A Wonderful Tree Bearing Tiny Lambs

There grew there [India] a wonderful tree which bore tiny lambs on the endes of its branches.

These branches were so pliable that they bent down to allow the lambs to feed when they are hungrie.[20]

Cotton Balls on a Plant Stem

As evidence, travel guides are always fun to read. Even now, travel brochures are nearly always better than reality, and in some cases, the reality can be downright scary. Despite government warnings people visit places that may be quite dangerous in terms of crime, economically depressed, and/or politically restless.

But sales must go on, so too in history teaching, seldom are questions asked about social unrest, pollution, air quality, or local theft and murder rates. We pay and visit anyway, playing travelers in a strange land, and we overlook the poor or the rebellious. But we have a problem and that is we are visiting "out of context" as time travelers and aliens. We need to know the inside story.

The story is what counts and we want value for our money. Some fanciful language with some spice added, and mysterious events and people, lure us into the new context. So, too, in past history, people loved reading tales of travel, real or imagined, and because knowledge was relatively limited, they more or less accepted the account as truthful.

The lure of the "other" is both a draw and a chance for seeing them as weird, strange, and frightening. Horror movies are a draw for much the same reason. The "normal" are worried about strange people who do not look or act like ourselves, and who may be dangerous. But we enjoy "exotic" and "unusual" up to a point, up to living with us.

So, we might say that Sir John may be "pulling our leg" is his tale of travel, or imitating ancient epics like *The Iliad*, or the *Epic of Gilgamesh* filled with both natural and supernatural events and creatures. We still love dragons, and griffins, at least in films and stories. Meeting one is another problem.

But returning to Mandeville, we might also be able to see that the stories arise from reality, perhaps with a great deal of misunderstanding, perhaps succumbing to playful tall tale-telling. There actually are places with tall "giant" people, and short "pygmy" people; there are "trees that bear wool" and what might you think those are? People without heads, mouths, or arms that is another story, considering what we know of human anatomy. Maybe that is going too far, but Sir Mandeville couldn't resist a good script.

But in reality, how might a medieval writer react to seeing a plant and its fiber that looks very much like something he knows, sheep's wool. A wool plant would seem quite wondrous. In the medieval context, this description communicates to what people knew, in ours we take products for granted. Few discoveries and marvels are left, alas. Perhaps that is why crowds are arriving on Mt. Everest, or surrounding the Taj Mahal? They want to see marvels for themselves.

V. AN INVITATION: CREATE YOUR OWN HISTORY CHALLENGE!

Rethink the history you know, and create or redesign lessons to fit a new format of investigations carried out with a suspicious mind. Facts should be checked even if they are called facts or evidence or data or information. Evidence is at the heart of history and the basis of historical writing.

Whatever description suits you or the authors and sources utilized, think like a detective. Don't simply accept the Internet or even a professional historian as a total truth teller. Question the notion of facts as truthful and create your own case studies to encourage students' critical thinking skills. Create an atmosphere in which checking facts, challenging assertions and theories, and justifying judgments are the daily normal way of doing things.

Perhaps you might like to think about historian, even by professional historians as open to question based on the standards we will apply throughout this volume.

a. Examining Historians' Claims

How historians handle and discuss sources goes very much to the heart of how we think about people and events, even into the future. In an era of controversy, fake news, and selective attention, the problems of history and the social sciences are greatly magnified not lessened compare to past times and places.

So, let's look briefly at the ways in which two historians handle their sources, each grappling with admissions about what is known and not known; each struggling with missing pieces from times long ago.

Adrian Goldsworthy presents a case study and history of the fall of Rome in a meaty and comprehensive book in which he notes,

"Two notable narrative historians provide detailed—and generally reliable—accounts Ammianus Marcellinus part of the fourth century and Procopius part of the sixth. Both were actual eyewitnesses to some of the events they described . . . other documents—mostly written on papyrus, but sometimes on writing tablets or pottery sherds, preservation has largely been a question of luck . . . It is vital to appreciate the limited amount of unequivocal fact discovered by archeology. All finds require interpretation, especially if wider conclusions are to be drawn. Any study of the ancient world is incomplete without considering the archeological record, but impressions drawn from the latter are liable to change as new discoveries are made or old ones reinterpreted . . . information is highly useful, but never exists in sufficient quantity to generate reliable statistics for population size, age range and the general levels of prosperity on more than a very local and short-term basis. All studies of the ancient world are forced to proceed without the support of statistics."[21]

Jack Weatherford weaves a tale of Genghis Khan across vast continents and cultures in a book of speculation and admiration in which he describes his subject,

"In contrast to this (negative) foreign perception, the Mongols have always seen Genghis Khan as their spiritual guide and religious teacher comparable to Buddha, Jesus, or Muhammad. . . . . God's commandment was simple: every nation must obey the Mongols. . . . Much of what we know about Genghis Khan's early life comes from a document known as The Secret History of the Mongols, written two years after his death. Someone, probably the chief Mongol judge SHigi-Khutukhu, gathered all the information that he could find about the man who had created their nation . . . the resulting text was a closely guarded treasure of mythic power. It was soon locked away. The manuscript belonged to the royal family, but they guarded it jealously, often even from one another, allowing copies . . . only when necessary, such as. To accompany one of them on the conquest of a new land. The document was written in a code that few people understood, and in time it was lost, only to be rediscovered in the nineteenth century and finally decoded in the twentieth."[22]

Each historian presents a discussion of their subject, that is, the Roman Republic, and Genghis Khan, discussing the topic and the sources used to develop a narrative for their respective books. Yet, each provides a contrasting scenario on handling the sources and drawing generalizations from them. Goldsworthy is far more sharing of the problems in dealing with past sources such as missing data, reliability of sources, eyewitness status, and the complexities of defensibly interpreting societies that existed a long time before us.

Goldsworthy shares with us the two ancient historians he draws upon who were also eyewitnesses to many of the events they discussed. He admits to the need for interpretation of sources, not simply their repetition and admits to the possibility of error because of insufficient data and gives examples of making educated guesses from sources about population, ages, economic conditions, and so forth. He shares the issues with us alerting readers to the problems historians face in developing comprehensive narratives that answer questions like, "Why Rome Fell?" The language used emphasizes drawing careful tentative conclusions rather than definite answers.

Weatherford also examines accounts used in developing a narrative about Genghis Khan admitting that his main source, the Secret History of the Mongols, was written a few years after the great Khan passed on. There is considerable language and retelling of tales about the Khan implying Mongols still see him as a hero, even if the outside world sees him as conqueror and savage warrior. He seems to side with the local, perhaps violating perfect historical objectivity in the process. Also, sources seem less clear and less contemporary with events than the Roman historian's sources. Some sources seem to be or border on myth and hero worship, including a secret code and hidden records, suddenly and miraculously solved in the twentieth century after 800 or so years of obscurity.

Thus, the two historians diverge in the willingness to accept or question sources, with one set of sources far superior in quality, the Roman, to the other, the Mongols. Historians need to share the issues with us, particularly an examination of sources for quality and quantity. They should also explain their own biases and preferably avoid joining their subjects in idolizing a hero especially one like Genghis Khan who is widely seen and was widely seen in his time as a brutal conqueror and destroyer of lives and property. A telling comment from Weatherford was that "God's commandment was simple: every nation must obey the Mongols." This command hardly sounds like the views of a benevolent leader and religious figure preaching tolerance for all religions.

Historians as human beings can also be swept away by their subjects and biases, despite a recognition of source issues and interpretation. This is what makes history and the social sciences so evocative and problematical, and beautifully teachable in a critical framework.

KEY QUESTIONS TO CONSIDER, APPLY, AND EVOLVE

- Why not build on the Mandeville travel guide by thinking about writing one of your own about "exotic" people and places, the "others"?
- Can you resist dressing places up a bit with good advertising?
- Can you be true to the evidence?
- Will you be frank about the negatives, if any, or too truthful about the positives?
- What if the natives speak a language you don't understand; will that help or hurt you as an eyewitness?
- What if you stay in a holiday inn the whole time: does that increase your experience of contact and understanding your new context?
- Is it easy or difficult to understand either the present or the past if you are "looking in" or "looking out"?
- Can we express both negative and positive feelings at the same time? Why or why not?
- What principles should guide you in examining evidence?
- What principles should you apply in reading and checking historians? Are these the same as the rules for everyday evidence?
- Should there be an overall philosophy to follow across time, space, culture, and people: Should you remain eternally attentive and suspicious or relax your guard?

NOTES

1. Oxford Online Dictionary. Retrieved October 24 March 2019.
2. Csikszentmihalyi, M. (1996). *Creativity. Flow and the Psychology of Discovery and Invention.* New York: Harper Collins.
3. U.S. Department of Education. (2017). Reimagining the Role of Technology in Education National Education Technology Plan Update. http://tech.ed.gov
4. Barton, K. C. (2005). "Teaching history: Primary sources in history-breaking through the myths" *Phi Delta Kappan* 86(10), 745.
5. Monte-Sano, C., De la Paz, S., and Felton, M. (2014). *Reading, Thinking, and Writing about History.* New York: Columbia Teachers College and the National Writing Project.
6. VanSledright, B., Kelly, T., and Meuwissen, K. (2006). Oh, the trouble we've seen: Researching historical thinking and understanding. In K. C. Barton (Ed.), *Research Methods in Social Studies Education: Contemporary Issues and Perspectives* (pp. 207–233). Greenwich, CT: Information Age Publishing.
7. Holt, T. (1990). *Thinking Historically: Narrative, Imagination, and Understanding.* New York: College Entrance Examination Board.

8. Seixas, P. (1993). "Historical understanding among adolescents in a multicultural setting" *Curriculum Inquiry* 23(3), 301–327.

9. VanSledright, B. A. (2004). "What does it mean to think historically ... and how do you teach It?" *Social Education* 68(3), 230.

10. Lévesque, S. (2008). *Thinking Historically: Educating Students for the Twenty-First Century.* Toronto: University of Toronto Press.

11. White, Hayden (2010). *The Fiction of Narrative: Essays on History, Literature, and Theory, 1957–2007* (R. Doran Ed.). Baltimore: The Johns Hopkins University Press.

12. Rawlinson, K., Wood, S. N., Osterman, M., and Sullivan, C. C. (2007). "Thinking critically about social studies through visual materials" *The Journal of Museum Education* 32(2), 155–174.

13. Wineburg, S. (2001). *Historical Thinking and Other Unnatural Acts: Charting the Future of Teaching the Past.* Philadelphia, PA: Temple Univ. Press. (Critical Perspectives on the Past) Paperback—11 May 2001.

14. Adapted from: www.teachinghistory.org (10 January 2011).

15. Passanisi, Jody. 2016. *History Class Revisited: Tools and Projects to Engage Middle School Students in Social Studies.* New York: Routledge.

16. Donovan, M. S., and Bransford, J. D. (Eds.) (2005). *National Research Council. How Students Learn: History in the Classroom.* Washington, DC: National Research Academies Press.

17. Felton, R. G., & Allen, R. F. (1990). "Using visual materials as historical resources" *Social Studies* 81(2), 84–87.

18. What is ephemera? (2011). The Ephemerra Society of America. Retrieved November 1, 2011, from http://www.ephemerasociety.org/whatisephemera.html

19. *The Travels of Sir John Mandeville, a version of the Cotton MS, in modern spelling.* (1900). London: Macmillan and Co., Ltd. Accessed at The Project Gutenberg, https://www.gutenberg.org/files/782/782-h/782-h.htm..

20. *The Book of John Mandeville, or, Sir John Mandeville's Travels, in Middle English, Illuminated Manuscript on Vellum* (from 1725 ed. The Voyage and Travaile of Sir John Mandeville, London: Reeves and Turner), Christie's, 2 June 2010, retrieved 25 June 2011.

21. Galsworthy, A. (2009). New Haven: Yale University Press, 24–25.

22. Weatherford, J. (2016). *Genghis Khan and the Quest for God.* New York: Viking Press, 9–11.

Chapter 2

Facts

Data as Information, Evidence, Stuff, Content, and So On

Everybody gets so much information all day long that they lose their common sense.

—Gertrude Stein

One of the saddest lessons of history is this: If we've been bamboozled long enough, we tend to reject any evidence of the bamboozle. We're no longer interested in finding out the truth. The bamboozle has captured us. It's simply too painful to acknowledge, even to ourselves, that we've been taken. Once you give a charlatan power over you, you almost never get it back.

—Carl Sagan, *The Demon-Haunted World: Science as a Candle in the Dark*

OVERVIEW

Facts raise issues about definition and verification for drawing conclusions in history and social science. Just how we decide on facts versus interpretations, or evidence and truth is the focus of discussion.

HEADLINE

"How lying and mistrust could take a lasting toll." *New York Times*, **November 10, 2019, B5.**

I. INTRODUCTION

We might begin with consideration of a definition of the term "fact" from an online dictionary, that is,

> something that actually exists; reality; truth: *Your fears have no basis in fact*
> something known to exist or to have happened: *Space travel is now a fact.* a tru th known by actual experience or observation; *I saw the church burn down.*
> something known to be true: *Scientists gather facts about plant growth.*
> something said to be true or supposed to have happened: *Napoleon rapidly conquered a vast empire but later lost it.* There are also legal facts. An actual or alleged event or circumstance, as distinguished from legal effects or consequences: *The facts given by the witness are highly questionable.*[1]

This definition of "fact" provides a rather lengthy and complex meaning for a simple word. These definitions cover a lot of ground ranging across existence, observation, events, and law, and this could be extended to more subjects. "Fact," therefore, is a multipurpose word with multiple meanings, some quite different if we migrate from one discipline to another, yet with overlaps and commonalities. The problem with using the term "facts" is its implication of truth. Statements of fact are easy to make and often left unchallenged but as we will see, fact can cover a multitude of meanings and a range of truths.

Real facts need supporting evidence and corroboration from several sources. In many cases, facts are definitions or conventions, accepted widely, but are not accurate data in the sense that we have proof. Dates, for example, are agreed upon by convention. Holidays are not often on the dates they were first conceived in history, and are decided by whosoever's calendar reigns supreme, that is, Latin, Greek, Jewish, Chinese, Iranian. Calendars are human inventions and differ widely.

We bandy words about quite blithely, but when you get to facts, there are many synonyms or near synonyms, such as data, evidence, and proof. This is our basic drawer of information, but all facts must be examined and interpreted to become useful. Just what constitutes proof of an interpretation or hypothesis isn't clear until you really work on your data, the stuff of which history is made. This "stuff," like a million-year-old "human" skull from South Africa, can arrive in many forms, sizes, and pieces, ranging from historical documents and archeological artifacts to film to poetry to art to music.

Depending on what questions are asked, data may just lie there uselessly, but in other circumstance for different questions, what was once useless becomes crucially important! Some data is "circumstantial" that is not completely convincing but based on the context. More data may be discovered that moves the circumstantial and partial to a better-supported interpretation of the facts.

For example, George Washington was the first president of the United States. This is a statement of fact that needs corroboration, which is available in many forms including records from the time.

These records are the documents of history and social science. George Washington was the greatest president of the United States as well as its first is a statement of judgment, and must lead to an evaluation of all presidents based on their merits measured according to established criteria for greatness, showing how the judgment was made in favor of George Washington.

It all depends on what facts you will accept and become conscious of in history.

a. Truth as Fact

The problem with "fact" implies that we have already settled on established truth, or that there is very strong agreement about what is true. In teaching social studies and history, we like to think that as teachers we are conveying facts, as truth, and this justifies the time put in on a subject. But the field is changing.[2]

Yet, this is a kind of low level of instruction focused on what, when, where, and who rather than which, why, and how, higher-level questions. Face facts, it is much more interesting to teach by asking questions than teach by giving (possibly inaccurate or biased) answers. If you think it is more interesting to convey facts then you can stop reading right now.

Facts can vary in meaning, as can all synonyms, information, data, inference, and judgment. These terms overlap, or supplement truth in different topics and contexts. Evidence can sometimes have the same meaning in history and law, for example, eyewitness reports are generally accepted and welcomed in both subjects.

The statement that "George Washington was the first president of the United States" is presented as a fact. There are many documents, speeches, and eyewitnesses, as well as paintings attesting to the truth of this statement. Also, it is offered as data, without interpretation or judgment. And it is not terribly interesting in and of itself.

The statement that "Weapons of mass destruction were built in Iraq" is also put forward as a factual statement. But we now know that there was no proof for this assertion and it was used by political leaders, including the president at the time, George Bush, to justify attacking Iraq, and replacing its regime.

Thus, on the face of it, factual statements may indeed be facts, but may also be false. We really cannot tell as historians and social scientists what is true or not true until we see proof, or at least supporting data.

But in law, only certain kinds of evidence are "admissible," that is accepted in court in support of the prosecutor or defense.[3] For instance, evidence that cannot be traced to an identifiable source, or that is passed to a second or third party, often called hearsay, may be ruled out of court as inadmissible in a particular court case. Historians usually agree with most of what a court would see as useful evidence, but legal definitions are much more particular and restrictive.

A good way of beginning any historical or scientific conversation is to review the concept of a fact. As you will note in the definition above offered in five parts, facts are assumed to exist in reality, or have been events that have happened, are known, or supposed to be true.

Facts may also be *alleged* to be true particularly if recounted by eyewitnesses. In law as in history accounts may *actually* have happened or are alleged to have happened, and may be true, partially true, or totally untrue, depending on the nature of the evidence in support.[4]

How many witnesses are presented and the extent of their corroboration is vitally important in law, history, and the social sciences. The nature of the witness' remarks is also crucial to proving a case or writing a strong narrative. A large number of eyewitnesses would offer stronger evidence than a few, while the education and intelligence of those witnesses might increase believability.

For instance, if witnesses from different backgrounds are in close agreement, that would strengthen a narrative or case. If they agree while representing varied ethnic and cultural backgrounds, educational levels, and locations that would further strengthen a narrative, and result in a more detailed story. By contrast, contradictory witnesses, or unreliable reporters, combined with partial or fragmented stories would diminish the trustworthiness of the evidence.

Actually, "fact" is a killer word in teaching and learning history which is, after all, about the evidence of past and present. Just as this sentence is ended with a period, it is past and we must attest to its creation by examining texts, but it no longer actually exists as it was first conceived and put on a page.

Much of factual proof depends on witnesses, recordings, and documentary evidence preferably from many different sources.[5]

b. Truth as Evidence/Information/Data

Data, or information, or evidence are much more neutral words than fact because none exude a sense of certainty or finality. Data like information defines a body of material that can be studied, analyzed, and organized into a story or proof of an assertion or claim about truth. Information is the stuff of life that requires study and processing to turn into something more understandable and meaningful data.[6]

Information/data can be used in many ways to test and prove explanations, theories, and to support judgments about a range of issues, like causes and effects, interpretations of actions, leadership assessments. How data is used can be very important but it is still seen as neutral until a hypothesis or judgment is put forward.

For example, crime rates may be going down, and we are not sure of the causes, but we are quite happy about this effect. We would like to know why the rate is falling, but we must first check how the information was collected and organized.

We may pose questions of the data, for example, Was the survey conducted by the police and/or by outside sources? How big was the sample?

Is all of the relevant data presented to researchers? Are trends clear?

What's missing, if anything, that is needed?

Have the charts and graphs been prepared to enhance understanding and does the information clearly demonstrate a fall in the rate consistently? If the data checks out, we can then challenge anyone who claims the crime rate is going up. We have the data to prove that assertion false. We possess the evidence to check or challenge any other assertions made about crime rates.

"Evidence" is also an excellent descriptive word for materials, eyewitnesses, and reports that provide the basis for drawing inferences and conclusion. But evidence goes further than information or data because it implies that there are rules for gathering information to test assertions about history and society.

Evidence also has a distinct legal meaning, that is, the materials needed to support a civic or criminal investigation. Court judgments have serious consequences to individuals and government because these decisions may result in penalties, charges, convictions, and imprisonment, or execution. Thus, evidence is vital to prove a case. Because of that, law codes usually prescribe and follow complex rules for the acceptance and admissibility of evidence.

Detective work to uncover evidence is legendary, and the work of both real and fictional detectives often centers on the discovery of evidence, weapons, DNA samples, corpses, and stories, that help the investigator make decisions about guilt or innocence, evidence determined whether a case can be built of sufficient strength to bring about a conviction in criminal cases. Civil cases work differently to some extent, but cases involving accidents, or payment issues, or property damage must also be supported by considerable evidence.

Historical investigation has often been compared to detective work, and there are many similarities indeed, the most important one being the relationship between investigator and the case, historian and the narrative. Both require witnesses, artifacts, careful study, inference, and theory to build a case. Both require evidence, corroboration, witnesses, and careful study of storylines.

In addition, history and legal cases demand considerable insight into the claims and personalities of the cast of characters in the case, story, or narrative. History and law differ in their rules for admissibility of evidence in determining truth, for instance, discounting "hearsay" third-party data, and favoring direct eyewitness accounts and lately biomedical data.

The law in criminal and many civil cases demands attorneys for the plaintiff or hearing officer, as for the prosecutor or defense, who act as guardians for their clients and each attorney cross-examines the other sides' data. This process works toward strong and convincing proof. The jury, if assembled, hears all sides to the story and makes a final decision about truth under the guidance of the judge, after listening to adversaries test and criticize the evidence available.

The quality of sources, mostly represented by witnesses and eyewitnesses are major sources of history, along with artifacts that include images, music, and films/videos, if available. The accuracy of eyewitnesses is very much a part of what we define as facts. An eyewitness who writes about a famous battle five years later is much less valuable than one who pens his account or films it while on the scene. Scientific evidence, artifacts, clues, forensic discoveries, add up to solid backing for what we call facts.

What, in fact, may be accepted as true, it may indeed be only a claim based on a few eyewitnesses. A good trial lawyer or prosecutor lines up as many eyewitnesses as possible to prove factual claims. Defense and prosecution cross-check each other, and the jury (that's you) with a judge's guidance decides which evidence to accept and which to exclude.

Facts also demand a context, a setting, and a set of rules for admissibility.

We may have contradictory accounts, disagreeable and unreliable eyewitnesses. Or we may discover that witnesses make up parts of the story, or are delivering an account for their own purposes, or to please a boss or overlord. We may have damage and deterioration in the written or pictorial accounts, lost parts, missing pieces.

Let's look *at the idea of facts*, which we may also term information, data, evidence, and primary accounts, meaning that the information we have was of the time, on or close to the event, consistent, from a relatively reliable witness, perhaps corroborated by one other witness at least. And let's think about facts as the stuff of teaching but stuff we can also call into question and check out.

If you cannot check and verify a fact then, sorry, it's probably not a fact but a mistake, interpretation, or invention. Questioning the facts can be confusing, exciting, and even humorous to students. But for teachers this questioning is the perfect opportunity to define and argue terms. The students get to

c. Truth as Story

Story and truth seem incompatible at first glance. Truth is factual, story is fanciful. This artificial dichotomy actually prevents teaching history in a thought-provoking way because there are only two poles to choose from, either accurate facts leading to truth, or made-up tales and fairytales seen as literary inventions.[8]

Nothing could be further from the truth than thinking about history as existing at the either end of two choices, fact or fantasy. This only works if you think history is bimodal and that good history leads to truth, the whole truth, and nothing but the truth. That actually happens rarely.

In real history, with all the warts on, there are all kinds of takes on truth as story, ranging from detailed lists of dates and names, photos of people, recounting of events to literature that beautifully tells a well-crafted tale.[9] There are a lot of stories in-between that are mostly, partially, or almost entirely factual, and true; and by contrast, there are stories that are almost entirely invented, partially invented, and almost mythology.

The idea of story ties the bits and pieces together, often in creative and entertaining ways, real and imagine, or both. The totally real story may be disorganized and confusing, told from multiple viewpoints. A good historian can review and retell the event in a way that makes the sequence clear and the characters vivid, leading to an explanation and/or interpretation of the story. The point is that power comes from the idea of a story and the eyewitness as well as the historian telling the tale to the best of their ability.

Reading fairy, folk tales and mythology can be very instructive for learning about past and present societies and how they thought about themselves and others. For example, you can read the *Iliad* or *Odyssey* of Homer many times and find out new evidence each time. Modern history and archeology can guess at the veracity of the details, but in some ways, it doesn't matter when creating a lesson: the more questions raised the better the story.

For example, if you read carefully, you will find that Cyclops is probably making Feta cheese in his cave from his sheep.

1. "We soon reached his cave, but Polyphemos (also known as Cyclops because he had only one eye in the center of his forehead) was out shepherding, so we went inside and took stock of all that we could see. His cheese-racks were loaded with cheeses, and he had more lambs and kids than his pens could hold. They were kept in separate flocks; first there were the hoggets, then the oldest of the younger lambs and lastly the very

young ones all kept apart from one another; as for his dairy, all the vessels, bowls, and milk pails into which he milked, were swimming with whey."[10]

The narrative of the *Odyssey* and *Iliad* makes many claims on modern credulity. But Homer nevertheless is a fabulous source for discussing technology, warfare, love, political rivalry, style, and foreign policy in a very ancient story. We don't actually know who wrote or where it was compiled or when it originated, but we can still take its message and descriptions seriously as both history and literature.

We can try to corroborate events through archeology but we don't have many written sources, and, most importantly, it is a tough case since we have no firsthand Trojan writers at all, no second hand either.

But we can learn from these ancient legends that there was conflict between two powers over a very crucial piece of property. Troy happens to be geographically situated near the entrance to the Dardanelles, the passageway to the Black Sea from the Mediterranean. This passage has been fought over for thousands of years Troy and the Greeks being the first written account we know of, with a cover story of a love affair that crosses borders.

How might we use the data on this map as "facts" to promote thinking about both ancient stories and modern? Examine the data and consider rules for settlement, and rules for trade. If you are choosing a site in this territory,

Figure 2.1   Sea of Marmara in Turkey. Wikipedia public domain/map from Demis. Map of the sea of Marmara. Bounding box West 26°, South 39.8°, East 30°, North 41.5°. Approximately 240 miles across from entrance to exit (now in northwestern Turkey): This work has been released into the public domain by its author, www.demis.nl. This applies worldwide/Wikipedia (September 2005).

what reasons or principles would you follow in making your selection? Do real-life locations follow your rules?

- What geographical features might be important in this bit of territory?
- Where on this map would you put Troy? Constantinople? Istanbul? Any important city? Why?
- Where would you put three cities of choice if you got to be their architect?
- Is this likely to be a valuable piece of property? Why or why not?

Love affairs across borders and cultures almost always make a good story, a story that also provide a lot of historical and geographic evidence about contact. It all depends on how we look at story or narrative as a concept, and at the specific account we are using as a source of information.

We can tie literature to history, and history to literature, partially or fully. It works two ways across a bridge between art and science, story and history. There does NOT have to be one final answer for teachers, nor does there have to be a division between fact and fiction. Really fine historical writing is literature, the better it becomes perhaps the less we can trust it for truth: it's an issue worth discussing.

When an historian puts a story together, the narrative tends toward a more neutral approach, than a literary creation. When writers have to tell a tale, in a style that can vary from simple and plain to complex and dramatic. All authors must deal with characters, detail, plot, action, climax, point of view, and narrator. Also, most fictional stories are based on lives lived and real experience, and cannot escape from a factual base.

The meaning of an historical narrative and of historical fiction can be quite similar or quite different, but all stories must follow a pattern of telling. And this pattern usually, most often, leads to a point or series of points that provide clues to cause and effect, interpretation, and meaning. How we read or hear the real story and the fictional story in terms of meaning and message are probably not that different. Each story and history narrative strives to offer us insight into different aspects of an event from varying viewpoints.

This is the joy, the fun, the detective work, in reading Homer (fictional/ historical), or Lewis and Clark (real/documentary), and making sense of their descriptions, attitudes, and reporting. Were the explorers' descriptions of Native Americans accurate and true or were their perceptions biased? Might their factual report be seen as story? There is no wall put up against evidence in either story or history, just that each is used in different ways to convey meaning and promote overall interpretations.

Think what would happen to any real story if Hollywood got its hands on it! Turning reality into fiction can be fun, and so can turning fiction into reality. Trouble begins when a witness says, "that . . . is not exactly how it happened," and a story begins to mutate into something different than reality. Even a documentary film can arguably be partly fictionalized simply by selecting and organizing the story into a better sequence or by enhancing some characters over others. Charisma in characters can be easily enhanced, and villainy made palpable in both history and story.

The story or the narrative can be "art-ed up" by using beautiful language or it can be reduced to simple and direct "factual" language. Nevertheless, there is still language and image, maybe sound and music, joined with insight and emotion embedded in all stories. Our species cannot escape its love of tales, myths, stories, history, day by day, and century by century. So, don't fight story problems, use them to stir discussion.

d. Truth as Inference

From facts, data, and information, we develop insights or inferences about meaning and message.

The data no longer simply lays there, but as we put pieces together it begins to shape ideas that help us to understand, to analyze, what we are looking at or reading. Inference is a word meaning that an idea or insight is drawn out of our studies, like reviewing a collection of prehistoric Stone Age pots, or chivalric documents from the Medieval period in Europe, or Shang Dynasty Chinese writing, or U.S. political cartoons before an election.

This contact with the evidence leads to a kind of detective-like investigation of the materials unearthed that produces hypotheses about meaning and message taken separately, and as a whole. Inferences, hypotheses, understandings are all labels indicating that reasons, explanations, and theories are beginning to arise from the data. These understandings and hypotheses help us identify causes and effects in history and provide insights into motives for human behavior.

The more data we can add to an investigation, the better and stronger we may feel about our inference/insight/hypothesis. In some cases, we think our insights are weaker, and unwarranted, based on the evidence at hand. Perhaps we need to return to our data at this point, adopting a new way of looking, focusing on a longer time frame, or a different theory.

We move beyond the typical schoolroom, "three causes of the civil war" to a deeper grasp of the ways slavery as a system impacted American culture in the past and well into the present. Perhaps we begin to see that a system begun in colonial times shaped the values of American society for better or worse over a very long period of time, not just since independence, and not just after the slaves were emancipated in 1863. We might take another look at Reconstruction and the Jim Crow era in the U.S. history, and then review the Civil Rights movement.

Long-range views begin to loom as more important than short-range views in understanding history, and that is an important step up from memorizing facts. This is a new stage of thinking, as we have risen above simply reviewing data and moved on to suppositions about purpose, message (if any), and how and why the lifestyles evolved.

We are now engaged in mid-level thinking rather than lower level of amassing information. We are ready to begin explaining the origins and purposes, the comprehension of objects, records, and actions. Perhaps you could label this using facts to refine and revise interpretations while organizing a search for new evidence.

Within a process of definition, for example, what is the function of an object, to cook, clean, bash, or drink, we begin to assign meaning to our discoveries. While giving meaning, we also add a sense of explanation: what something is "likely" designed for and how we can identify and defend our interpretation of its style and function.

We move from the discovery of several thousand-year-old clay pots to the notion that the vessels are probably, most likely, drinking vessels, or cooking vessels. We may not be completely sure but we think there is a pattern to the look of the objects repeated across a culture. The vessels appear analogous to pots and vessels still in use that have the same shapes, more or less, and we extend our analogy to build explanation.

We may also find new data, dried liquids within the vessels. We can test remnant traces within a pot of water, milk products, wine, cheese, olive oil, or some other liquid. This gives us further support for our increasingly clearer inferences about design and purpose. We go up the scale of critical thinking into middle and higher realms of discourse. Facts become part of a chain of reasoning that coalesces around a hypothesis or theory that gives meaning to the vessels.

We realize that we can sort pottery styles into categories for different purposes, across different kinds of food and drink. Then we add our analyses of the materials and styles used to construct the pots. We are getting closer to broad inferences about the technological skills and needs of the culture as a whole.

Thus, fact-finding based on the analysis of archeological, historical, and social science discovery, grows into a more comprehensive grasp of a culture's lifestyle and level of accomplishment. We have used our facts, evidence, and data to create an elegant and probably valid understanding of the past, building analogies to present-day lifestyles and technologies to interpret ancient pottery styles and uses.

e. Truth as Evaluation

As soon as someone says, "I am simply and truthfully presenting the facts," your ears should perk up and your brain come alive with the word "suspicious"! Simply and truthfully (if you can define both) itself implies a value judgment applied to the evidence as easy to grasp and accurate. Look out!

Contrary to popular opinion in teaching and learning, facts need to be verified and sourced, then judged as more or less trustworthy, more or less proven. Not only must evidence be evaluated, but primary and secondary sources may be rife with judgments about people, places, and events.[11]

The nice part of truth as judgment is that there are key giveaway words used to express evaluations, for example, assess, estimate, judge, appraise, worth, quality, good, and evil. These are value words. Although we all want honest, accurate, and verifiable history, economics, and politics, the entire field is riddled with opinions, judgments, and assessments.

Just as most bottled brand name waters come from the same taps (if you research their points of origin) so too does evidence and information need to be tracked to their sources. As teachers rarely have the time to check their facts to the source, they often rely on tertiary textbooks as sources. Everyone should exercise caution about accepting factual assertions. Assertions have the upsetting quality of sounding exactly like factual claims, maybe with false claims overlooked.

But you can and should practice pre and post-mortem diagnostics on the evidence.

Textbooks are generally written to sound neutral and trustworthy, believable, comprehensive, and meaningful. Passages sound authoritative but are actually based on primary and secondary sources that may be inconsistent and contradictory.

Classroom general texts in history tend also to be behind the times in terms of the work of historians who seek to update and correct historical narratives. It would be better for all of us if teachers and students learned how to choose and test primary sources on their own without leaping to tertiary summaries.

Textbooks also tend to suppress controversy and clashing ideologies because they want to do business across the nation and are risk averse to value positions and judgments. Textbooks may suppress or hide their agendas and avoid controversial positions on many topics. Taking a stand, or even setting up and identifying "sides" in history, can be bad for sales across states with blue-and-red voting populations. This is one of the reasons that race, class, and gender are avoided or treated gingerly at best, or at a distance.[12]

In fact, it is almost impossible to tell the difference between a fact and a claim, unless you question the sources. People, particularly in media, say a great deal about the news, and offer claims that are frequently unsubstantiated. Hearsay evidence is not admitted in most courts of law, but the media are only restrained by their readers and libel laws, neither of whom necessarily recognizing what should or should not be questioned.

Issues with competing "sides" and conflicting philosophies can be a huge challenge in deciding which claims are really factual and which are false or fake. Sometimes the facts are correct, but so skewed, so selected, and so incomplete, that they are difficult to verify or criticize unless you are expert and knowledgeable on a historical and political topic.

II. SOURCES AND PROVENANCE

a. Introduction

The concept of a "Source" is a label applied to the original locations, dates, and author accounts of historical material, whether in the form of artifacts, narratives, documents, or images. There can be many sources in many genres from the past and present, and we can test and add these together to develop an insightful narrative or story of events. Many more and better sources lead to more trustworthy overall histories and social analysis of past and present.

b. Primary Sources (Authentic to a Time and Place)

Sources that originate or purport to originate from the time and place they were written are usually referred to as original documents, that is, contemporary with an author's life and times. These documents can take many forms, images, things, documents, and historical accounts of the time, perhaps by professional historians of the day.

Authors, eyewitnesses, reporters include writers, composers, artists, artifacts, news accounts, speeches, all manner of firsthand evidence. In a sense, these are not facts as truth but rather the foundation of what we see as facts inside a document proving that an historical figure was really there at the time.

In many cases, the primary documents prove to give us deep insight into life and times that are past. It may be easier to study the relatively fewer past sources than the altogether too and too prolific busy present.

Sourcing should be a first since the contents of the reports are needed before we really get around to asking more difficult questions. Fact questions should be simple, of course, who, what, where, when, but sometimes it isn't, and you have to chase a source around quite a bit hoping you will find the "original."

It might be a translation, or it could be a forgery, or worse yet be taken from an Internet website, "www.anythingyouwanttoknowabouthistory.com": But check to see if sources are identified. If not, then how do you find out who the author may be? So, yikes! This could be fun and result in something like trying to catch gophers with a fishhook.

The big question about sources should be whether we approach them with a sense of *open-mindedness, or a predetermined outlook or ideology.* Teachers should approach sources with an open view, of course, one that does not yet privilege any interpretation of viewpoint, and avoids a particular ideological interpretation, though that may indeed be useful and close to the truth, for example, a Marxist interpretation of a revolution.

Beginning with a particular theory or philosophy may preclude the detective work necessary to carefully study the evidence. But we do need guidelines to know what we are looking at and what we are looking at.

Claim-evidence connection is awkward, but important, and this is a second step up asking for checks on claims. In other words, can we use the evidence discovered to build links to the claims eventually made about the meaning of events? Are we still collecting and analyzing real-life events for the *documentary film under way, or have we already proceeded to add, shape, and edit the story into a satisfying drama?*

For example, is there proof of slave ownership, and do we have authentic papers or records to prove ownership? In other words, how do we prove what is said or written or shown? Evidence checks on claims, and holds the promise of keeping everyone busy checking facts, false news, and outright lies by reviewing everything everyone says or does not just as facts but as "claims" to truth. "Claims" has a kind of nice nineteenth-century gold rush feel to it, (is there gold there and is it real?). You might also raise questions about "claim jumpers" and fool's gold.

Analysis of primary sources is a vital historical step toward making sense of the contents, as primary sources are indeed the basis for building claims, creating interpretations, and drawing inferences about historical cause and effect. A document, image, film, or song does not in itself tell you what it means: that takes work and detailed combing of the evidence for clues, understanding, and conclusions.

Analysis has a nice weighty feel to it like we are sharing sources with a chemist or psychiatrist who will give us insight into motivation, message, and meaning, and the pursuit of "truth." We might even be able to develop a formula to interpret the content! Key to analysis is the tension between and among sources, *seeking corroboration over conflict*. We hope to find sources that reinforce each other in terms of story, characters, and time, but, alas, history is full of examples where sources conflict and clash in both facts, claims, interpretations, and overall ideologies.

The process of sorting conflicts and finding corroboration is basic to historical thinking. Often sources clash and conflict while we seek agreement, and we have to learn how to try to make sense of the antagonistic claims.

Multiple accounts and perspectives lead us to the all-important concept of corroboration and questions of reliability and validity, *on a scale from very diverse to solid conformity.*

Key questions might include,

- How do we know witnesses are telling the truth, and how do we establish rules for the admission of evidence?
- What if there is only one bigoted eyewitness, or two that contradict each other, or three that tell nearly different stories?
- What if all the witnesses have an agenda, an ax to grind, a perspective that may shape, edit, and distort reporting of the historical "facts"?

Oh no, we have more than one view to deal with, maybe too *many views all conforming to the same story from suspect sources.*

What about having experts go over all the evidence for us, you know, historians, political scientist, sociologists, and the like? The professionals will all give the same diagnosis and treatment no doubt, and we shall be saved from thinking for ourselves, hurrah! But hold on here, the historians and social scientists and archeologist differ *holding diverse views.*

They often don't agree on how to interpret the evidence, worry about missing pieces, inaccuracies, bloated claims, and willful theorizing. This is like being in a fifteen-car pile-up on Route 80, and examining the police reports to find out who caused the crash: result, no fault insurance.

Therefore, we particularly treasure corroborating sources that have no self-interested agenda in particular to prove anything or support anyone. For example, most of what we know about Jesus comes from the tales of his disciples, but these are interested parties actively lobbying for converts to believe in Jesus.

A corroborating source is the Roman noble, Josephus Flavius, who was Jewish, left us an amazing account of relations between the Roman Empire and ancient Israel. Josephus book, *War with the Jews*, mentions Jesus of Galilee confirming his existence and a hint of his activities at the time.

c. Testimonium Flavianum

About this time there lived Jesus, a wise man, if indeed one ought to call him a man. For he was one who performed surprising deeds and was a teacher of such people as accept the truth gladly. He won over many Jews and many of the Greeks. He was the Christ. And when, upon the accusation of the principal men among us, Pilate had condemned him to a cross, those who had first come to love him did not cease. He appeared to them spending a third day restored to life, for the prophets of God had foretold these things and a thousand other marvels about him. And the tribe of the Christians, so called after him, has still to this day not disappeared.[13]

d. Secondary Sources (Summaries of Primary Sources)

Secondary sources are works about the *firsthand materials* of history and social science, the eyewitness contemporary observers and reporters. The narrator, usually a historian, or social science writer, studies the original documentation and ties it together into a story, with sequence, characters, causal factors, and often an evaluation of people and events. A professional seeks out and identifies the witnesses and artifacts that are the basis for analysis and interpretations that seek to explain actions and reactions in history.

History writers, biographers, or documentary filmmakers carefully collect, check, and compare the evidence to create a defensible story of people and events. This can be quite difficult for many reasons, particularly if there are controversies, conflicts, and confusion. Documents may have passed through many hands, with additions, deletions, and alterations, not clearly identified. To work toward a balanced and fair account, the historian needs many different viewpoints and reports, and must include contrary views.

Another problem arises if there is either an overwhelming pile of evidence, much of it trivial, or too little evidence with a great deal missing and/or biased. Modern life since Internet tends to provide too much material to deal with efficiently, as in emails and reports, news feeds, and so forth, much of which is repetitive and banal. So, the social scientist or historian must seek out and select what she deems most useful to develop a narrative. Government news can be managed, edited, and even deleted to reflect well on whoever leader is at the time, so takes special effort to choose carefully what really matters.

Overall, as we approach and meet our present, the spewing of words increases across websites, newsfeeds, government agencies, new programs, tweets, emails, and paper books and articles. In many cases these are repeats and rephrasings of each other, leaving the writer of secondary narratives with tough choices for sources that she can trust. Selectivity becomes an issue as does searching for the origin of a story or viewpoint. And there must be tests for bias as well.[14]

The other side of the coin is too little evidence. Delving into the distant past for secondary sources may yield relatively few summary accounts of times and places, that is past historians and authors who have told tales, their interpretations, of a past distant to them. They are closer to the actual events than we are, but much may have been lost or converted to legend and myth, often difficult to separate out.

Much more use of artifacts and art may be necessary for ancient or prehistoric studies. For example, Homer's *Iliad* or *Odyssey* yield a great number of clues to life in Mycenean Greece of 3,000 or 4,000 years ago, but this is in story form and it is difficult to date.

Portions may have been added or lost in the two epics, and there is clearly a strong propagandistic strain in favor of the Greeks, although their opponents the Trojans are not belittled as enemies. That would not be fair, and it would make it seem way too easy for the Greeks. By the way, from a modern point of view, there was no nation of Greece at that time as far as we know, although there was a collection of Greek-speaking political entities.

e. Tertiary Sources (Overviews of Most or Many Sources)

Tertiary sources are defined by textbooks and reports that seek to integrate both primary and secondary sources into an overall narrative within national history, and world history. Textbooks are usually aimed at schools, often secondary through college, and attempt to summarize and explain both the reports of primary writers from their times and secondary writers, usually historians. These authors attempt to build comprehensive pictures of entire nations, regions, continents, and global events. This is a daunting task!

Textbooks and online sites like Wikipedia can be very helpful in organizing and integrating vast amounts of information, data, and evidence with the analyses of historians and social scientists. A great sweep of history can be offered in these books, replete with scholarly analysis of the causes and consequences of actions.

But there are drawbacks because these narratives may lack detail, and may oversimplify causes and effects in an attempt to reach a high level of understandability. Writing Big History is very difficult because so much has to be covered and integrated into a coherent whole.

Thus, historians and philosophers, social scientists and scientists, must be consulted and their theories fairly explained. In their search for a grand narrative that explains how we got where we're going is difficult to achieve particularly if we commit to a balanced approach that does not privilege any nation or empire or give only one nation's viewpoint.

For example, the current expanding concern for our global environment requires deep historical analysis of our current predicament. A few conceptions of the world's story have been offered but there relatively few comprehensive explanations of climate change or ecological degradation. This will undoubtedly be attempted in the near future, and requires a vast knowledge of the sweep of climate change, combining science with history.

There are also "tertiary account" problems of bias, and problems of fairness, omission and commission that may skew a long-range analysis and require revision as new data and new finds appear in history. Throughout recent history, there is a trend toward what is sometimes called "global" or "big" history, tertiary summaries of primary and secondary accounts used to build a vast but efficient view of the world's story.

Big overviews can be very exciting in providing new views of historical action and change, but may also challenge one's sense of comprehension especially if the reader is unfamiliar with the base materials. Adding up and integrating many world historians and a vast data base of evidence into a comprehensive view or review of all of history can be great fun, but also reducing the history of many peoples to mere footnotes.

Big sweeping stories need a center and organizing idea that ties many details together, and this demands a scholar with wide knowledge and a critical eye. The last fifty years or so have produced a number of outstanding world historians and social scientists.

Nevertheless, we are perhaps at a point in time where we need grand-scale analyses of global history, and there have been many attempts with interesting points of view. For example, there are environmental histories, like *Something New Under the Sun* and *The Green History of the World* that attempt to review global history from an ecological perspective.

There are also global narratives from a species point of view, woman's point of view, as well as liberal, radical, and conservative perspectives on offer. Tertiary narratives try to retell the history of the world from a theoretical framework that explains the course of events and perhaps boldly offers a judgment on where we are headed in the future.

III. CONTEXT: TIME AND PLACE, MEMORY CONTINUITY, LOSS, AND COMPARISON

a. Introduction

Historical memory is said to be based on facts, but actually is based on a process of filtration from sources to interpretation through narrative or story.

How the story is written depends on the writer, producer, director, and artist, if such are involved. But someone or in the case of texts, a partnership or committee, determines the content, and the message.

Historical memories are determined by sources, but these sources are products of a time and place, a period of peace, turmoil, boom or bust, and social, economic, and cultural factors influence how the facts survive and enter our memories.

States, nations, and political entities are critically important in keeping facts alive as memories. Often these facts are used to send other kinds of messages, conveying cultural superiority, a literature of complaint, social criticism, national pride, or a statement of who counts in history. What facts are important at one time may be changed or fade away at other times.

Who is important to study as president of the United States may shift as the society changes; which women are promoted for study may shift with the winds of feminist criticism. Even who is worth reading in literature or history can shift dramatically as the context evolves.

Memories are usually based on facts but these may be dramatically changed by shifting forces in a society.

b. Context

Context is where, when, and with whom we find ourselves. It surrounds us like a wall and we absorb its values, speech, and knowledge. We are inside a dome of information and others are outside the same dome, but this is changing with the worldwide expansion of the web. Contextual grounding gives us a sense of being somewhere and reminds us of who was there with us or our ancestors. The highest levels of context provide settings, weather, character actors and actresses, and emotional states. If you can smell the focaccia baking in ancient Pompeii then you have context and a recipe!

In our present day the electronic marvels of the Internet, the web, the iCloud give us more and more data across all systems, and it is harder and harder to tune out the "noise" of communication.

What governments and individuals do not want to hear or have others hear can be closed down and hidden from the masses. Governments can play BIG BROTHER to use an Orwellian phrase. Tuning in can be easy but our initial contact may become overwhelming, as we are inundated, deluged by a tsunami of information, opinions, views, values, and news, much of which may not be true, and much of which may yield no significant conclusions. Sorting out the ordinary from the important becomes a vital skill. The tsunami effect makes reflection more difficult and the sheer size of the data pile can make us throw up our hands in dismay.

But a good historian, political scientist, or economist trooper on, perhaps cutting out a small bit of data to dig into carefully and critically rather than biting off more than can be digested. But context too is dangerous especially if we are inside a privileged, patriotic, and controlled information flow. The more privilege, patriotism, and control, the less sure we can be of the quality of our data or the reliability of our conclusions, much less the value of our values.[15]

To mitigate the envelopment in a context, we must seek outside knowledge, alternative knowledge, and ask a lot of questions about sources, interpretations, and feelings expressed in every aspect of historical and social scientific knowledge. We seek knowledge from other news media, preferably not our own, say BBC or Al Jazeera, or underground and above ground blogs providing alternative views to government issue. These folks may provide us with the sensory context of a time: how people look, where they are, what are they listening to, who do they see as heroic or cowardly, nasty or beneficent.

Achieving a real sense of context is a tall order and makes for tensions, but tensions can be useful in driving a lesson forward by raising issues of trust, trustworthiness, reliability, and validity. Can we be sure of what we know if we are accepting only officially mainstreamed, sanctioned interpretations of daily life, past or present? Even the concept of history itself may need debate and discussion. We begin to grasp detail about other human's lifestyles, woes, and problems, rather than ethnocentrically focus on our own above all others.

Context immerses in the details, sounds, sights, and smells of the world around us at the time:

We begin to understand why ISIS exist, why the Pharaohs wanted to be worshipped as Gods, what Romans ate for lunch, how Vikings built ships that could survive thousand mile voyages, and we begin to see humanity in the context of needs and wants that have to be satisfied to sustain a community of human beings on the move.

c. Continuity and Exhaustion of Memory

Quarrels about Facts as Memories

Our species is quite remarkable in terms of memory storage. Minds can collect and file vast amounts of data in great detail. Then they can just as easily suppress, confuse, or bury memories.

Our ancestors could keep track of many animals and plants, habits and movements, as part of the job of hunting and gathering. They were very sensitive to environment and could probably predict weather (we need a TV to do so). But there are trade-offs between long (organized and updated by repetition) and short-term (working) memory, with short term being shunted toward long term as time goes on. Thus, the human memory shifts and changes, so we needed records, pictures, and calendars to help remind us of events and people, but these are imperfect.

Then there are psychological processes that block or mix or suppress short-term memory, and sometimes bury long term so deeply that special icons or associations are needed to draw out the information. Emotional attachments to memories tend to burn those into more easily accessible files, while boring lists and data collections tend to be suppressed or moved into long-term storage.[16]

In teaching and learning history, most teachers, for example, spend a lot of time helping students to memorize "facts" such as names, dates, and places, quickly learning that these are most easily forgotten. Since much of this factual data has little or no relevance to students, they forget very quickly. As well, many teachers prefer to avoid topics and stories that have strong effects on people, and particularly controversial, troubling, and deeply held emotions. Thus, history is not everyone's favorite subject, at least not as presented in many typical fact-laden courses of study.

Within homo sapiens' grasp are a great multitude of memories, mostly very personalized, and evocative of meaning. But decay in long-term memory and the human tendency to rewrite stories toward a happier, and more satisfying ending, with greater style than substance on occasion, and you have history mutating before our very eyes. Written records are more easily analyzed and checked than spoken or played or painted simply because language is more efficient at conveying content, meaning, and message.

But all factual reports should be subject to analysis aroused by suspicions of forgetting, rewriting, conforming, and emotional selectivity. If you agree these are problems not just of history but of all human memory, then the admonition to beware in believing historical records must be taken seriously, indeed.

d. Memories by Fact and Invention

Very often, history is manipulated in images and words using popular media, especially newspaper images, stories, and photos or films. The media itself may suggest historical themes and interpretations, and if these pictures become well known, iconic, then others can hop on the bandwagon and alter the meaning and message of an image. It is important to remember which media first introduced a message to the general audience in order to understand how subsequent images will use or reinterpret the medium.

Photographs are a people's art form as the species likes to view images, of themselves, others, exotic places, major events, and so forth. There is a thirst for images but to use them properly teachers need comparisons and questions to direct attention. Remaining suspicious of intentions and revisions can help us focus on the image and its context, as well as the possible or probably intentions of the photographer.

Here below, we have two famous images produced by different artists one year apart, the first in 1912 and the second in 1913. Both have to do with a theme of labor and industrial work, and both portray children at work. Since pictures are usually taken for a purpose to remember people, places, and events, we immediately must ask ourselves what the picture taker may have deemed important enough to click the shutter. After all, the boys in the photo are quite ordinary, maybe even poor (notice one doesn't have shoes) and they are doing ordinary work (probably spinning).

What are they making and why are children allowed in a weaving factory? Why aren't they in school or at home or out playing?

We must place the picture in social context: perhaps there was no school, perhaps these kids are working after school, perhaps 1912/1913 was not like "now," and perhaps we better investigate labor and working conditions. Let's also consider how viewers of the time might view the image; with approval or disapproval or indifference, and why? We might also raise questions about the industrial revolution, so called, and really carefully eyeball the kids and the factory. Let's raise some questions about these pictures:

- Is the factory well organized and clean?
- Are the boys clean, and of the same social class, and what might that class be called?
- Are the machines dangerous looking? Might the boys have to be careful?
- What exactly is their labor?
- What might their Mom and Dad think about sending them off to the factory?
- Let's get personal: would you like this job and for how long?
- Would the photographer want us to ask these questions or others?
- Does the artist of the poster below remember the photo above: how can you tell?
- How does this poster compare to the previous photo? Which is real? Which is imagined and how can you tell? Does the historical source matter: poster by artist or photo by picture taker?
- Why or why not?
- Who is in the poster: boys or girls or can you tell? Is the poster like the photo or different?
- Might the poster have been designed for some purposes, and if so, for what purposes?
- How is the "Boss" shown: what is he wearing, standing on, and why is he shown at all? Why are there money bags near the bosses' feet? And why is the boss fat? Are the working girls fat?
- And why does a quote appear, stating that "the worst thief is he who steals the playtime of children" and who is W. D. Haywood? And why might you join the I.W.W?
- Does the Boss appear in the photo? How does the boss change the meaning of both the photo and the poster?

Figure 2.2 Children at Work in a Cotton Mill, 1912 (Photograph of Children in Factory). Library of Congress Photo/1912 ID 4974.

- Does the poster have more or less of a message and meaning, stronger or weaker, sharper or duller, than the photo? Who and why has the message of the photo been reshaped and to what end?
- Why and how does the artist remember and reshape the photo? Which picture is more powerful in your opinion? And can you explain which picture is likely a more reliable account of history?

IV. CORE PRINCIPLES

In conclusion, let's take a look at a summary of historiographical rules for inquiry. Any one or two of these rules is enough of a focus for a lesson. Use sparingly and deeply. Avoid trying to accomplish too many at one time or anytime. Stick to the two you choose and dig for evidence while encouraging students to create hypotheses to accept, reject, and modify.

Core principles proposed for determining reliability and validity are shown below. Any single rule would be enough for an entire discussion in a classroom or group. More than two or three would be enough to organize a unit of study, and the entire list might last an entire year or more. Case studies and

Figure 2.3 Thief—An IWW Poster, 1913 (Engraving/Poster). IWW International workers of the world courtesy of The Smithsonian Institution/Washington, D.C.

examples can be tested against any and all of the rules, in recurring cycles, that give deeper and more lasting meaning to history and the social sciences.

All sources are valuable for constructing social and historical meaning but original documents and artifacts tend to form the base for further analysis and inference particularly in joining a range of different and opposing eyewitnesses to test hypotheses and explanations.

Human sources may be relics or artifacts such as a fingerprint or a mummy; or narratives such as a statement or a letter or a government announcement. Relics are sometimes more credible sources than some narratives, but narratives give a great deal more knowledge across a wider range of emotions.

Core principles of source criticism were recently reformulated by two Scandinavian historians, Olden-Jørgensen and Thurén (these have been adapted and expanded by the author).[17] Following is a list of core principles to apply to any and all of history, cross time, and space:

- Any given source may be forged or corrupted, edited or transformed. Strong indications of the originality and authenticity of a source from the time increase its reliability.
- The closer a source is to the event which it purports to describe, the more one can usually be trusted as accurate historical description of what actually happened. But a proviso must be added that the source's trustworthiness may be compromised by an author's culture, politics, role, class standing, ideology, and/or religion.
- An eyewitness (particularly if corroborated) is more reliable than testimony at second hand, which is more reliable than hearsay at further remove, and so on. However, a professional historian may produce a more valid account of an overall event than those of the time by assembling and testing all available sources.
- If a number of independent or "outside" sources contain the same or a similar account, the credibility of the message is strongly increased.
- A source may be suspect if it displays or infers a hidden agenda or motive for providing some kind of bias. Suspicion may be minimized by, or supplemented with, documents with opposing or divergent motives that counterbalance accounts.
- The more emotion expressed by a source in its account may cast doubt on its reliability but may also increase insight into how people felt about events of their time.
- If it can be demonstrated that the witness or source has no direct interest in creating bias or supporting any particular view, then the credibility of the message is increased.
- Secondary sources that show how primary sources were used to construct hypotheses are more valuable and meaningful than secondary generalizations that fuse facts and documentation in ways that are taken for granted to formulate hypotheses.
- A combination of sources, primary and secondary, as well as tertiary textbooks written by professional historians and social scientists, may be more powerful at explaining events than any single original or secondary source.

KEY QUESTIONS TO CONSIDER, APPLY, AND EVOLVE

- Are there any rules you might add to the list above?
- Which three rules do you think are most important in history and social science? Why?
- Can a false or fabricated source yield historical information as well as "true" sources?

- How would you judge eyewitness accounts?
- Do historians by and large present reliable interpretations of events?
- Would emotions in a source, primary or secondary, make you suspicious or increase the value of the source? Why?
- How much information, and from which sources, would be enough to make a defensible conclusion you can trust? Explain.

NOTES

1. Dictionary.com, "Fact," accessed January 20, 2021, https://www.dictionary.com/browse/fact?s=t.

2. Stearns, S. (July 30, 2019). What Changed: in Social Studies Education?

3. U.S. Federal Evidence Review. (2010). web.archive.org/web/federalevidence.com/rules-of-evidence.gov

4. Loftus, Elizabeth F. (1996). *Eyewitness Testimony* (Revised edition). Cambridge, MA: Harvard University Press.

5. Shafer, R. J. (1974). *A Guide to Historical Method.* Illinois: The Dorsey Press; Tosh, John (2006). *The Pursuit of History* (4th ed.). Pearson Longman.

6. Brundage, Anthony (2007). *Going to the Sources: A Guide to Historical Research and Writing* (4th ed.). Wheeling, IL: Harlan Davidson, Inc. (Chesney, T. (2006). *An Empirical Examination of Wikipedia's Credibility* (3rd ed.). www.firstmonday.org issue 11/11).

7. Gilbert, J., and Garraghan, G. J. (1946). *A Guide to Historical Method.* New York: Fordham University Press.

8. White, Hayden (1987). *The Content of the Form: Narrative Discourse and Historical Representation.* Baltimore and London: Johns Hopkins University Press.

9. McCullagh, C. B. (1984). *Justifying Historical Descriptions.* New York: Cambridge University Press.

10. The Odyssey, Book Nine, stanzas 307–359 Homer [1932]. *The Odyssey of Homer.* Translated by Lawrence, T.E. Oxford University Press.

11. Müller, Philipp (2009). Understanding history: Hermeneutics and source-criticism in historical scholarship. In: Dobson, Miriam & Ziemann, Benjamin (Eds.), *Reading Primary Sources. The Interpretation of Texts from Nineteenth and Twentieth-Century History* (pp. 21–36). London: Routledge.

12. Harris, L. M., and Girard, B. (October, 2014) "Instructional significance for teaching history: A preliminary framework" *The Journal of Social Studies Research* 38(4), 215–225.

13. *Flavius Josephus: Antiquities of the Jews*, Book 18, Chapter 3, 3 based on the translation of Louis H. Feldman, The Loeb Classical Library. http://www.josephus.org/testimonium.htm

14. Marwick, Arthur (2001). *The New Nature of History: Knowledge, Evidence, Language* Houndsmills, UK. Palgrave/Macmillan.

15. Howell, M., and Prevenier, M. (2001) *From Reliable Sources: An Introduction to Historical Methods*. Ithaca, NY: Cornell University Press.

16. Eysenck, 2012.

17. Olden-Jørgensen, Sebastian (2001). *Til Kilderne: Introduktion til Historisk Kildekritik (in Danish)*. *[To the sources: Introduction to historical source criticism]*. København: Gads Forlag.

Chapter 3

Bias

Human Prejudice and Feelings of Superiority

A man without a bias cannot write interesting history—if indeed such a man exists.

—Bertrand Russell

There are many humorous things in the world; among them, the white man's notion that he is less savage than the other savages.

—Mark Twain, *Following the Equator: A Journey Around the World*

OVERVIEW

Bias, prejudice, unthinking, and subconscious feelings are the center of attention in this chapter across issues of class, race, gender, patriotism, and ideologies. All will be considered as potentially important in warping our sense of history and society.

HEADLINE!

Artificial intelligence is learning everything from us, including biases. *New York Times.* November 12, 2019, B 1+5

I. INTRODUCTION

"Bias" is a short word that encompasses a dozen or more meanings, but basically revolves around what *Webster* defines as, "prejudice in favor of or against one thing, person, or group compared with another, usually in a way considered to be unfair": there was evidence of bias against foreigners: synonyms: prejudice, partiality, partisanship, favoritism, unfairness, more antonyms: objectivity, fairness, impartiality.

Is anything left out in your view of the idea and meaning of bias? Would you prefer a narrower or a broader definition of bias in history?

a. Personal Taste and Preference/Likes and Dislikes

Bias is about likes and dislikes, ranging from personal taste, for example, "I like strawberry flavor and you like chocolate" to class and ethnic prejudices, for example, I hate gypsies (Roma) and their music. At the personal level, the choice arguably has consequences of marketing value, but does not involve social or political mores.

Once we move into the realm of social and historical bias, we have raised the idea to a much higher and broader level, one that affects immigration or neighborliness or denies choices to others. A social bias has far-reaching consequences for gypsies, known as Roma, that may result in social opprobrium, exile, and persecution.

This is still a bias of relatively limited scope directed at one ethnic historical group who are seen as "different" in terms of race and culture. If the bias expands to all Roma, then to all nomadic peoples, then to all brown or black people, then to all speakers of "foreign" languages, we are running into big trouble historically and culturally.

Deep and wide prejudices are a kind of bias that leads to political, economic, and social exclusions. Punishments and discrimination can multiply and harden hatred and conflict between and among peoples. We are not yet even at the door of tribalism or its larger version, nationalism.

b. Best and Better than You and Yours!

Bias can expand to encompass group and community values designed to raise pride and exclude "others" who are different in some ways. Such differences can include appearance or race, language or even just dialect, and unfamiliar customs. Depending upon the way a people, tribe, or nation is viewed, prejudices can range from relatively mild to very strong and hateful.[1]

People are contradictory and can be friendly as a community but also hostile to members perceived as strange, aggressive, and different, holding on to customs unlike the dominant group or majority. A sense of superiority leads to viewing others (the unlike) as strange, inferior, and alien. In many sci-fi films, aliens are often horrific creatures blasted away before getting a chance to show any intelligence or human qualities. They have to exterminated, even if their technology is superior, and they have not behaved aggressively, in order to save the human race.

In some cultures, opposing or competitive groups are viewed negatively almost from first contact, much in the manner of team spirit where one side is viewed as "ours" and the other as "theirs." Cooperation is trumped by competition. And competition can follow rules that keep aggression and bias within relatively humane bounds but can mutate into open violence on occasion when one side is seen as suspicious, hostile, or unpleasant. Bias explodes rapidly if one side does not kowtow to the power that sees itself as superior to the other side.

c. Insiders/Outsiders

A vitally important issue in social science and history is humanity's need to belong and also its need to exclude. "Belongers" know their culture, the advantages, the sources of pride and work, the local lingo, and customs. They tend to overlook the internal problems and the negatives. Adopting insider viewpoints as "truth" without looking at outsider viewpoints as well, results in very poor history. Cultures are imagined and have internal customs known mainly to the "natives."[2] It is much like forgetting to ask for a second opinion before surgery. What if you receive two very different interpretations to cut or not?

Outsiders come and go, but the longer they stay the more attention they must pay to adaptation to the dominant culture and its contradictions. Every culture, by the way, has contradictions: for example, the ideal of many cultures is that "all men are created equal" but when we get down to who has rights, some (think class, race, and gender) seem to have more and better rights than others. Even a familiar subculture can present problems for the biased, especially if that portion of the population is a majority or sizeable minority.

Once outsiders elect to join the common culture, they must deal with language/accents, social customs and mores, as well as working to make a living. Every culture has rules of entry, formal and informal, and every culture can pretty much tell outsiders from insiders. It takes a lot of know-how and learning to join a "foreign" culture fully and completely.[3] How many of us could ever do that?

Points of reference for outsiders and insiders can produce very different interpretations of people and events, with insiders excusing or overlooking certain kinds of bias, while outsiders feel hurt and rejected. Within a society with different groups of insiders, the same biases can have a very hurtful, maybe even more hurtful, effect than for true outsiders.

Here is one point where historical interpretations demand feedback from both insiders and outsiders on people, places, and events. Otherwise we have only one-sided views and reports that are suspicious! Prejudice may preclude treating the outsider views seriously or may make the insiders quite angry and fearful. Sometimes, insider/outsider clashes prevent belonging, and reject efforts to belong. There are many historical tragedies of clashing cultures that never quite understand each other, often with devastating results from underestimating the potential for payback and conflict.

d. Identification/Self, Friends, Family, Tribe, Nation, World

Finally, building identity is a fourth factor in adopting biases toward the "other."[4] Yet people cannot live without identity of some kind, even if it is a common culture, bland and mild-mannered adoption of central values not taken very seriously. Identification and identity are complex affairs: a mix of personality, culture, faith, history, politics, class status, gender, race, and family.

This mix can produce generous, welcoming people who understand differences and make allowances for others, or may produce narrow-minded insiders who view all others as outsiders to be wary of on a daily basis. Much depends on the state of the economy, political leaders, local conditions and mores, religion, and historical development as a whole. The mix and attitudes can also shift dramatically in the hands of different leaders and the rise and fall of an economy. The self is a product of many factors including friends, family, tribe, subculture (if any), nation and world. This increasingly wider world approach to growing up can vary significantly with time, place, gender, race, and personality.

Friends and family do the socialization bit, and if local contacts are monochromatic, then attitudes may be more restricted and biased than if local contacts are diverse and toleration rules the cultural context. Oddly, small differences, think North and South, between insiders may cause more rivalry and conflict than very great differences with outsiders.

Much depends on the status of outsiders, for whom identification is swift and often either strongly negative or mildly accepting. Zulus meet British in battle, German, Russian, and British royalty meet each other in drawing rooms; the Dalai Lama meets the Pope, and so on. A good way to test the boundaries of identity is to go into history to look at cultures in contact, and arrange meetings between leaders, settlers, and citizens, then look over the results.

II. DIFFERENCES

Although differences exist within the singular human species, actually there are far more similarities in behavior and belief. Differences yield more drama than similarities, and also make it easier to act in a prejudicial manner toward "inferior people."[5]

We all share personalities, walk mostly upright, and hold identifiable emotions we can mostly recognize. Of course, you might argue that this depends entirely on your viewpoint and biases! If you want to regard another nation as subhuman, inhuman, or partially human, that is your privilege but it is unlikely to lead to good relations or help your understanding of history.

It is quite clear, and always has been from Neanderthal times, that we humans are a single species otherwise we could not breed together and mix races and genders, cultures and histories. The species goes back a long way, perhaps a million or at least a half million years since we have scientific data that most of us share a bit of Neanderthal or Denisovan genes, if not others who disappeared as recognizable residents.

Similarities are often given less attention than differences because differences (and conflict) are more dramatic and yield a frisson of excitement. To think you are only human, no more, no less, is a bit boring and lacks dynamic interchange. It implies life is conventional and conformist, whereas an invasion of different people is exciting if troublesome, and invading others can be an exciting exercise in domination and control.

Yet we are all rather similar and with worldwide globalization becoming more so all the time. We dress and eat and act so much alike in much of the world that it is harder to identify who is whom or where is when in published photos. Historians can argue that. Globalization has been in progress since humanlike creatures left home in Africa and crossed into the promised land in West Asia, also known as the Middle East. By the late twentieth and early twenty-first century, most people are wearing the same clothing, pretty much, same symbols, if any, and fight over much the same issues.

We are one big worldwide species riven by biases and keen on noticing differences.

a. Appearances

How we look physically, particularly on issues of race and gender, is one major source of historical bias.

However, appearances can be deceiving since much of humanity has been "mixed" from time immemorial, regularly joining with other peoples, or separating, depending on political and geographic circumstances.[6,7] Inbred and isolated populations often develop distinctive cultures and patterns of speech and appearance because the gene pool has remained pretty constant, maybe! We now have genetic studies and can identify inheritance of genes, which often comes up with surprising conclusions.

Those who think they are "pure" should be very careful what they wish for since that is a code word for bias. Pure what? Why are there so many blondes in Russia and the British Isles, for example. When the English persecuted the Irish, they depicted them as monkey-like, that is, subhuman. Yet, modern genetic studies indicate that the Irish may be more Scandinavian than the English who are more Gaelic than the Irish! Whoops!

Appearance often focuses on only a few indicators of importance, and those are skin color, facial features, and hair, maybe height. Hair and skin colors are built into languages across the world, identifying the biases in cultures some of it almost at the unconscious level, la blonde, la brunette, le noir. These are the first features we notice, and depending on culture and upbringing, politics and a sense of inferiority or superiority, we rate the other as insider or outsider. Dress as well as face and body may determine reactions, especially when one group is well-off and the other poor.

At times height and build can be important and this too is genetic. Humans evolved in different environments and adapted to them accordingly over thousands of years. Thus, different people developed bodily mutations adapted to cold, warm, sun, distance, and food supplies. Skin color, and appearance, is a social construct of distinctiveness that is actually on a sliding scale of color and size and shape and features. In English, we even give an inappropriate name to a people as "Polynesian," meaning multiracial, of many races, and probably could barely tell Pacific Islanders apart if we and they all wear the same blue business suits or dresses.

A fine example of bias is the Roman's view of the invading Huns, who the historian Ammianus Marcellinus, an upper-class Roman, described in less than flattering terms in AD 374–376 from his comfortable vantage point within the empire's borders. He offers readers of his time the following description of the barbarians as,

> the people called Huns, slightly mentioned in the ancient records, live beyond the Sea of Azov, on the border of the Frozen Ocean, and are a race savage beyond all parallel.

> At the very moment of their birth the cheeks of their infant children are deeply marked by an iron, in order that the usual vigor of their hair, instead of growing at the proper season, may be withered by the wrinkled scars; and accordingly they grow up without beards, and consequently without any beauty, like eunuchs, though they all have closely knit and strong limbs and plump necks; they are of great size, and bow-legged, so that you might fancy

them two-legged beasts, or the stout figures which are hewn out in a rude manner with an axe on the posts at the end of bridges.

They are certainly in the shape of men, however uncouth, but are so hardy that they neither require fire nor well-flavored food, but live on the roots of such herbs as they get in the fields, or on the half-raw flesh of any animal, which they merely warm rapidly by placing in between their own thighs and the back of their horses.

They never shelter themselves under roofed houses, but avoid them, as people ordinarily avoid . . . as things not fitted for common use. Nor is there even to be found among them a cabin thatched with reed; but they wander about, roaming over the mountains and the woods, and accustom themselves to bear frost and hunger and thirst from their very cradles. And even when abroad they never enter a house unless under the compulsion of some extreme necessity; nor, indeed, do they think people under roofs as safe as others.

They wear linen clothes, or else garments made of the skins of field-mice; nor do they wear a different dress out of doors from that which they wear at home; but after a tunic is once put round their necks, however much it becomes worn, it is never taken off or changed till, from long decay, it becomes actually so ragged as to fall to pieces.

They cover their heads with round caps, and their shaggy legs with the skins of kids; their shoes are not made on any lasts, but are so unshapely as to hinder them from walking with a free gait. And for this reason they are not well suited to infantry battles, but are nearly always on horseback, their horses being ill-shaped, but hardy; and sometimes they even sit upon them like women if they want to do anything more conveniently. There is not a person in the whole nation who cannot remain on his horse day and night. On horseback they buy and sell, they take their meat and drink, and there they recline on the narrow neck of their steed, and yield to sleep so deep as to indulge in every variety of dream.

And when any deliberation is to take place on any weighty matter, they all hold their common council on horseback. They are not under the authority of a king, but are contented with the irregular government of their nobles, and under their lead they force their way through all obstacles. Sometimes, when provoked, they fight; and when they go into battle, they form in a solid body, and utter all kinds of terrific yells. They are very quick in their operations, of exceeding speed, and fond of surprising their enemies. With a view to this, they suddenly disperse, then reunite, and again, after having inflicted vast loss upon the enemy, scatter themselves over the whole plain in irregular formations: always avoiding the fort or an entrenchment.[8]

Not only is the Roman historian, a professional by the way, describes the Huns in prejudicial language and provides a near caricature of the Hunnic appearance and lifestyle, but he does give them due respect for their toughness and warrior abilities. Even newborn children apparently are marked by vigor but are described as "two-legged" beasts, not very complimentary to say the least.

Nevertheless, despite the bias displayed by Ammianus, we can gather important information and we discover they are nomads who live on their horses and with their animals. They are loosely governed and counsel each other in a kind of horseback democracy. The Roman sees them as not really ruled by a king of their own choosing. Roman prejudices are quite evident and much of it is directed at customs but also at appearances. The Huns appeared as the very quintessential invading barbarians to elite Romans.

b. Customs

Each group and culture, nation and people, has its own distinctive customs that are part of "insider" knowledge, and build insider identity. Customs often involve specific kinds of food, music, art, films, dress, speech, and social behaviors. Polite behavioral rules are laid out in most cultures and to reject those is to go beyond the bounds of good taste and proper behavior.

In some cultures, customs demand quiet and respectful speech, clean of swearing oaths, others may identify themselves by being loud and direct; still others quiet and reserved. There are customs along all of these lines of conduct, with rules espoused for public and private actions. What may be common and tolerated in one place is shunned and condemned in another, leading to the formation bias and accusations of boorish or uncouth behavior.[9]

Still other customs relate to rites of passage through life and cultures tended to organize recognition from birth, to coming of age, marriage, and funeral practices that identify allowable and approved social expressions of joy and grief. Some customs, like weddings, have crossed many cultures and now are nearly universal like the fancy white wedding dress. Others, like funeral rites, can still vary widely as customs for burial and remembrance within different cultures.

Heroines/heroes, sports teams, political leaders, and movie stars are also part of customs about who we honor and celebrate, who we teach about in schools. Cartoon heroines, or heroes, can play a cultural role imitated and honored almost as though they are real. Wonder Woman and Batman are favorites, though Wonder Woman is really an immigrant from another time and place, created from a "race" of Amazons who were part of ancient Greek mythology.

The Wonder Woman cartoon story generates a double sense of "other" across gender and culture, history and status, yet seems easily grasped and believed. Underlying the tale are serious questions about social values and historical recognition, not to mention the sexist thinking of Greek Gods.

Customs extend across the whole range of daily behavior and have become more alike across nations and regions, as globalization proceeds to homogenize and diffuse ideas, artifacts, and practices across most cultures. Foreign films that present different customs are more tolerated at least by that slice of the populations across the world who are willing to see films made by "others." U.S. films are recognized across the planet, even when clashing with local customs and beliefs, while acting as a homogenizing agent for most people.

c. Language

Language is a complex issue since a particular language is identified with some cultures, while other cultures freely switch between and among languages. Some language *and* cultures are dying out, or have been decimated, while others are making a case for becoming worldwide speech. Even within linguistic groups across many nations, languages can vary in pronunciation, spelling, and expression, for example, there are varieties of Spanish, English, and Chinese, depending on location and tradition. Some Americans have to turn on their translator for British cockney but not for Downton Manor aristocrats.

In the nineteenth century, the so-called Age of Nationalism, many nations were virtually identical to their languages and their cultures, fixed tightly in national boundaries. Close identification with a single language that is imposed upon all citizens of a society tend to be associated with narrow thinking and theories of superiority over others. The enforcement of a dominant language, single official language, or form of speech has been a source of considerable conflict within many societies, and is not always handled diplomatically within a nation, leading to a great deal of argument and sometimes outright armed warfare.

Empires, by contrast, have often included multiple languages, cultures, and peoples, and have by and large been tolerant of the mixing of groups and numerous spoken tongues. The Romans did not extirpate the languages of the conquered but they did spread Latin as a unifying means of communication.

However, many empires and nations have also encouraged or demanded that the peoples within, of whatever origin, speak also the language of the conquerors or dominant group, excluding or disallowing local dialects and languages from official approval, such as being taught in school. Spain has had serious conflicts in history by its minorities over giving Catalan or Basque official status as well as their own Spanish. Big trouble results from nations or empires that try to suppress minority cultures and their languages, often leading to revolts and terrorism.

Allowing many languages and cultures to bloom has almost always led to peaceful interaction rather than the clashes set of by restricting second or third language practices.

d. Belief Systems/Religions

Belief systems can have a deep influence over how people describe and react to their world. This includes reactions to nature, people within and outside the culture and polity. Belief systems mostly deal with faith and religious values, but can extend to political and social philosophies that create worldviews. This may be extended to include ideologies and political philosophies like Communism, Fascism, Liberalism, and Conservativism as well as others.

Such belief systems influence almost every aspect of daily life often providing or creating rules for dealing with power, money, and treatment of other peoples and classes. For example, most faiths have strong rules regarding charitable behavior in particular and morality in general. Belief systems offer a philosophy of life to their followers and sympathizers, a view that should be built into all historical and social science study. After all, such religions as Christianity and Islam or Buddhism over comprehensive ethical rules on almost every subject.

Beliefs about class, gender, sexuality, and race may profoundly affect social relations and may reshape the faith itself in surprising ways. Slavery in the United States before the civil war was justified and attacked using the Bible as a major source of reference. Claims about beliefs may be at variance regarding the overall tenets of a religion, even countering the moral teachings of its founders. Nevertheless, belief systems broadly influence nearly every aspect of life, and if a society identifies itself with one philosophy, faith, or political ideology, that tends to seep into every realm of life.

A world of caution is called for when we approach religion since the systems cover a great many peoples and time periods, and change accordingly, or not, but may include branches, sects, subgroups, and oppositional breakaways. Thus, religions and ideologies are complex, deep, and diverse, not easily characterized in a few moral precepts. If you are an outsider to another faith, then you should approach this by emphasizing their own texts, or by offering both insider and outsider authors and reporters of original sources. Since there is conflict between faiths long past, and up to the present, special caution is required.

Islam, for instance, for centuries historically increasing contact with other peoples and places, can be presented very negatively in some parts of the world, causing wonderment about why so many people are embracing the faith. Misreading of religious texts, hostility, and personal prejudice militate against an easy and honest presentation of Islam by a non-Muslim. However, all faiths would be best presented first by insiders. Let's at least get a grip on the ideas and beliefs from "their" viewpoints before we apply any of our own value judgments.

Belief systems are integral to most societies, shaping mores.

e. Fears

Since time immemorial peoples have been born and raised in one place and then moved on to other places, but usually only after a period of socialization that created a local culture. How long a culture or society is settled in a location determines its level of inbreeding and a portion of its suspicion of outsiders. After going walkabout, the locals have contacted other peoples and places, sometime with sociable results and other times with antagonism and violence.

Much depends on context and conditions encountered, according to social scientists that determines fears about others. Isolated and inbred groups tend to treat foreigners with reserve and a sense of anxiety about change. But a complex of values, like that of religion, promote good treatment of "strangers in your midst," perhaps offsetting negative feelings.

People who bond into families, bands, and small groups tended to be wary of "strangers," but not necessarily hostile. Hostility begins with the reinforcement of local cultures and the growth of boundaries. Even nomads, however, had food supplies and territorial patterns to defend.

However, as groups settled and became more territorial, at least in theory, they grew more defensive and suspicious of others. So also did other groups and competition began leading on occasion to conflict, violent conflict. This may explain the beginnings of warfare. However, as groups also moved around seeking foods in nomadic fashion, there was relatively little conflict.

With the advent of agricultural boundaries, borders, fences, and walls, property becomes more valuable. With large and more populous settlements, and the rise of surpluses, protection of property became more essential. There was also a growth of local cultural beliefs and styles, with differences becoming more noticeable between settlements. As farmers united into communities, the state developed in all its glory and what were local cultures became drawn into a larger, more unifying culture, language, and belief system. Rich states had to both defend their territory fending off other powers, while becoming more aggressive themselves.[10, 11]

As cultures, groups, and states formed more distinctive features and beliefs and territories expand, others seem quite a bit more divergent than before. State and tribe tend to reinforce differences rather than similarities to serve their growing economic interests and to build support for an internal culture. As the world has developed from hunting to agriculture to industry to state and regional systems, with the rise of nations and empires, competition arises on a larger and larger scale, and wars become more devastating with new technologies.

All of this produces fears and anxieties about "others," about inequalities, about control of environmental conditions and resources. Fears are often exacerbated by the news media, the state, and political groups. Thus, fear rises and reason falls, though there may be little or no actual conflict to witness or report.

Fears about others, and a sense of anxiety prevent or distort our approach to and grasp of history, rendering diplomacy more difficult.

III. CODES

Codes are clues to historical meanings and messages (mostly in symbols, words, or actions) that may be covert or overt or somewhere in between. They are sometimes called "codes" because their value may not be explained directly. We may look at a picture, for instance, or a symbol, like a flag, or a song, and overlook its meaning or misread its importance. We may also perhaps misinterpret intent and agenda.

Historical documents include a great deal of information that has implications for race, class, gender, culture, and provide entrée to political identity or philosophy, and national pride. Virtually, every document can be discussed using these same social science concepts as guides to thinking and asking questions.

In some cases, codes can focus on just one or a few meanings, while others like politics, ideology, and patriotism may be closely bound together.

a. Race

Codes about race can range across a spectrum from subtle to explicit, but always refers to a combination of factors such as skin color, facial features, body and hair. As a concept, race has been used to cover a multitude of peoples, many of whom would not be classified as a race even by racists.[12]

Since all humans can intermarry and produce children, race as a concept clearly has largely social and cultural meaning rather than only biological importance. As a metaphor for difference, many cultural groups have been portrayed as biologically different from their conquerors or oppressors, while in fact they may be of much the same genetic origins.

Race is a strange invention, serving political and social purposes when needed to persecute or grab wealth or land from "others." The Irish were treated horribly by the English and racialized though both peoples were clearly Caucasian. Differences were actually ethnic and religious, but Irish were downgraded by defining them as a race.[13] The struggles between English and Irish in the eighteenth and nineteenth centuries led to portrayals that were racist in tone and character especially by English artists who regularly depicted "Paddies" as monkeys with odd hats.

For centuries the English looked down on the Irish, seeing them as foreigners speaking a different language, social inferiors, and Catholic fanatics. Irish peasants were often portrayed in tatters, begging, and looking somewhat monkey-like with odd, "Paddy" hats. The English, by contrast, viewed

Figure 3.1 "Spare a thrifle, yer Honour, for a poor Irish Lad to buy a bit of—a Blunderbuss with a." *Source*: J. Leech. Wikipedia public domain English cartoon, 1842. John Bull symbol of England and an Irishman wearing a "Paddy" hat.

themselves as above the Irish, neatly dressed, speaking the correct language, and well-off. A sample may convey English bias better than words. Note the class privilege displayed, the poverty of the Irishman, and the caption under the cartoon. Each figure symbolizes bias, including the fat Englishman dressed formally mimicking the British symbol of John Bull, and the Irishman subservient and poverty stricken wearing out-of-style clothes and a drooping "paddy hat," no doubt green in color.

Decades of deeply racist set of cartoons was clearly meant to signal that the Irish were less than human and boorish, while English overlords were civilized and completely human. Both peoples as are all peoples of the British Isles are closely related genetically. The differences are linguistic, ideological, and cultural yielding a racial view of one related people to another.

If this type of view can develop among related peoples, where does it take us when facial and skin features and color are far greater?

b. Class

Social class is another factor we like to look for and assess in teaching history as this often yields important clues to rifts within societies, and yields corresponding biases. Dress, style, speech, and finances are all part of the codes we use to judge the class to which someone may "belong" when we take a look at them.

This is a highly inexact science, however, based on appearances alone, particularly since worldwide dress patterns have converged. The business suit and the dress have become nearly globally adopted, cutting across race and gender and nation (with some exceptions). Gone are the glorious days of noble status clothes demonstrating clearly what level you belonged to so others may perform the required obeisance.

Gone too largely are folkloric clothes that tell us where you may have originated and which culture you were part of in those days. So, nowadays we have to ask questions subtly about status, and notice petty details of a person's dress, like, "what a lovely watch you're wearing: is it a Rolex?" Or, blah, blah blah, you own an eleven-room mansion in the Hamptons, wow.

Saudis, for example, still wear their traditional dress thereby allowing easy identification of ethnicity but not so easy about discerning class level. Thus, unless we can look at bank accounts or notice how much cash someone is withdrawing at the ATM, we must look at subtle clues of address, zip code, jewelry, style, and speech to determine class standing.

We also tend to think in stereotypes or sociological terms to describe class status, being stuck with upper, middle, and lower, or white collar and working class, or aristocracy, bourgeois and proletarian. Nevertheless, class is a key part of historical interpretation, and requires investigation and judgment in determining status based on pedigree, money, or family, which could provide powerful explanations for behavior, for example, during a revolution or election campaign. For instance, we need to examine how class and race and gender determine voting patterns.

c. Gender

Sex and gender have a great deal to do with bias, and biases can run in many directions. But the big one is the divide between men and women. Each society has its own set of rules or codes on male and female status, marriage patterns, behavior, and the distribution of wealth and power. In some cultures, this has been complicated by newly emerging tolerance for and admission of cross-sexual or multiple sexual identifications.

Sexual relations may be further complicated by codes for sexual preferences, class status, and economic wealth. There may also be strong cultural values and codes in how the sexes are supposed to behave in relation to the society's values and to each other. Thus, gender goes very deep influencing the way history is recorded and who acts in the role of recorder.

History is clearly deficient in promoting the history of women by themselves, or within the context of the culture as a whole. The lower status of women, and the problematical roles of women in writing history holds across all the cultures of the world. Only a few societies have achieved an egalitarian approach to the status of men and women.

LGBT segments of the population need more discussion in history but may be hard to identify because much of this existed underground. The social sciences are perhaps a little more advanced than other subjects in treating women's issues and in having women join the discussion but there is still a long way to go in equalizing the scholarly input and output of women vis-à-vis men in the disciplines.[14, 15]

Gender cuts very deep into understanding historical events, people, and places because there is such a shortage of documentation by and about females, and certainly by and about LGBT communities. In many eras and societies, women are virtually absent as reporters, authors, leaders, and cultural icons. They exist only in their limited and limiting roles as mothers, wives, and mistresses, a big problem to correct by teachers.

Teachers really have to look around to find women in history, not to speak of heroines or villainesses, for that matter. Gay and lesbian views and characters are just beginning to emerge, but have not become widely included in standard textbooks. And teachers need to be sensitive to codes that lower or impugn female status, power, influence, and importance.[16]

Thus, we need to be particularly careful about considering the roles of women in history in relation to men, as noted by a leading female historian of our times, Gerda Lerner,

> The effect on men has been very bad, too, of the omission of women's history, because men have been given the impression that they're much more important in the world than they actually are. It has fostered illusions of grandeur in every man that are unwarranted. If you can think as a man that everything great in the world and its civilization was created by men, then naturally you have to look down on women. And naturally, you have to have different aspirations for your sons and for your daughters.[17]

d. Culture

Returning to culture, there are many codes to follow that in the minds of the denizens of that society are "theirs," a shared part of local customs and mores. All members of the common culture were brought up with these practices, symbols, and activities and almost instinctively know their meaning. Sports, like the ancient Mesoamerican ball game, or American baseball can reinforce cultural identification.

Foods and dress are also part of a common culture, even though these items may have evolved or been borrowed from other cultures but, nevertheless are thought of as uniquely French, Indonesian, American, or German, or Chinese, like "French fries, Satay, Hot dogs, and Sauer Kraut, and Wok stir-fry."

There may also be "cultural heroes and heroines" from the arts, film, music, and literature who provide a sense of prestige and accomplishment to the group from which they arose.[18] Most members of society are familiar with important national characters, either through schooling, literature, media, or government and private benefactors. Famous authors, songwriters, and movie stars may form part of cultural identification. Musical forms, song and dance, folklore, and historic figures may also be used to build identity and recognition.

The more widespread the recognition, the more powerful the associations with the common culture, and the greater the potential for bias by members against those who wish to revise and expand historical traditions.

Criticizing famous culture heroes may cause considerable discomfort and recrimination or even violence. On the contrary side, minorities and women figures may be left out of the conversation and be almost unidentifiable unless teachers insist on looking into a figure who is important and fun to study. For example, take a look at Mother Jones, a labor leader in Chicago as an example of those who are "left out" yet deserving a second look.

Thus, each society promotes a culture uniquely its own, with its own subtleties that take an outsider time and socialization to recognize, thus serving as a test for insider/outsider status. As cultures mix, and immigration patterns change, the combination of cultural identity shifts. Change may be welcomed in some cases, like hello to Mexican foods across America, but goodbye to illegal immigrants from Central America.

Biases and prejudices are often quite contradictory in nature and deserve study.

e. Patriotism/Ideology

As noted before, each culture, nation, and political movement promotes codes to build loyalty and create identification with the body politic, and/or dominant ideology and philosophy. Even in ancient times, peoples and empires created symbols for themselves, identified with gods and goddesses, recognized and honored important leaders. They (and we) build and built stories about themselves and their society that would become widely adopted by all segments of the population.

In some cases, loyalty to the state, and familiarity with its official culture, were nearly identical, in other situations state and society are separated according to the political and social conditions, for example, democracies, dictatorships, monarchies combined with languages, art forms, and education.

Patriotism, love of country, from love of city-state to love of empire and monarch, prime minister and president, have cemented many cultures of diverse peoples together to build a community that shared values and political preferences. This could be enhanced by the spread of a common philosophy of government, and/or by religion, as well as by language and literature.

The mechanisms of state usually employed standard textbooks telling the nation's story preferably from a positive point of view. Likewise, educational materials, traditions, and historical figures were honored and/or created to impress their accomplishments on citizens. Popular recognition of those making contributions to society were presented in a way that built identification with a national or imperial concept of the state. Even coinage and money could be used to serve state interests not just economically but also symbolically.

Identities in many states and empires could cross cultural lines to encompass diverse peoples and places around shared values if not shared ethnicities and language. Much depended on how socialization was handled, by rewards

Figure 3.2 American Half-Dollar with the Motto E Pluribus Unum, from the Many, One. Photograph by Jack Zevin.

or by force, or by a mixture of methods that produced and supported a national identity, like schools and cultural institutions.

Symbols and codes were signs of a shared belonging to an entity designed to govern, defend, and extend power. The state and government were also supposed to create and sustain economic opportunity for all or most of the citizens.

For example, the eagle has a glorious history of being handed down as a shared symbol from ancient Rome to the Byzantine Empire to Germany and Russia and the United States.

The American half-dollar with the Latin motto "e pluribus unum" or "from the many, one" also holds a "fasces," a reed bundle symbolizing unity.[19]

This noble raptor was a fitting symbol of empire, whether of a Republic or a monarchy, and is an example of the historical evolution of codes through thousands of years. The Roman codes still apply after thousands of years with the eagle as a favorite. In Middle Eastern cultures, the lion tended to be the central symbol of power and leadership. Talk about animal and flower

Figure 3.3 Eagle of the Roman Republic Holding Lictor and Fasces, Symbols of Rome.
Luis Garcia Zaqarbal, July 9, 2005/GNU License under Wikipedia.

symbols with your students and help them understand the reasons behind these identifications.

Codes also include items like flags, songs, sports teams, colors, and heroines/heroes to emulate and honor. The more common and shared the figure, the greater the symbolic importance of these cultural links across potentially divisive issues like class, race, and gender. This also presents code issues such as how do you choose symbols for female figures who were not warlike and while promoting freedom and liberty, did not act as aggressors on anyone except the largely male politicians who denied them entry to the vote, business, and political office.

IV. THE HUMAN CONDITION: INFERIORITY/SUPERIORITY

Bias, prejudice, and ethnocentrism are at the heart of understanding human behavior, as humans have evolved in history into a highly social species capable of both cooperation and conflict. Now conflict and cooperation can take place on a grand global scale indeed.

A great deal of the interaction depends on environmental and economic conditions combined with which social, political, and religious values are emphasized within the group, whether a band, tribe, nation, or empire. Groups that develop open and welcoming values tend to get along better with others but may also misread other, hostile, groups. Hostile groups may take what they want from others, but must eventually learn to live with each other and others as they settle down. This pattern of constant jockeying for position with regard to treatment of others has likely persisted since the dawn of time.

On the whole, groups do not like living in conditions of either anarchy or oppression. Anarchy and/or oppression produces a flight syndrome, and many try to escape to greener pastures, more peaceful places, if they can, if they are allowed admission. Joining another group, a society, is not as easy as it looks either for the migrant or the member. Membership always has a price!

Biases emanate from both directions, the insiders and the outsiders, and can range from mild preferences to outspoken hostility. A new cultural adaptation and construct can take a good deal of time, energy, and money to accomplish anywhere in the world.

A major part of global and local bias is prejudice against others (whoever "we" are and "they" are) that seem "different," or appear different, or follow "different traditions, speak other languages." This type of prejudice operates to put diverse groups "in their place" and make them feel like second- or third-class citizens, or classify them as noncitizens. Being great and superior makes conquest easier and produces more docile and cooperative society.

There have been multicultural and diverse societies in the world's history, and most of those have been quite successful by pretty much leaving the different groups alone, but requiring obeisance to the dominant group. The Persian Empire of ancient times, the Romans, Austria-Hungary in the nineteenth century, and modern America and Canada, have created diverse societies composed of a mosaic of cultures rather than a single uniform civilization.

Within these states and empires, there are still problems of prejudice based on race, gender, class, and perhaps religions. Deep prejudice arises when lines are drawn sharply between races and genders, or between cultures and classes. Codes of admiration and attention indicate who is on top and who below, and a relative lack of attention indicates who is marginal or looked down upon. Prejudice reinforces each aspect of status by either emphasizing differences or accepting them, with quite different results for societies.

Historical understanding increases as bias is controlled, or at least openly admitted, and adjusted for in reviewing people, places, and events.

a. Institutional/Political Partisanship/Power

Political dominance has been a goal for many peoples, nations, and empires, seeking to extend their power over ever larger groups. The powerful have a problem, however, in achieving control if they are biased in favor of a particular philosophy of life or political system. A commitment to a system that they try to impose upon others seen as practicing inferior systems and views leads to complaint and rebellion about second-class citizenship for some groups.

While politics is a part of bias, power relationships can provide cover for conquest by incorporating captive peoples into the overall system and socializing them into becoming supporters of the regime in power. Power and economic services can be used to socialize peoples, immigrants, and subcultures into a state as loyal citizens who adopt the dominant values, language, and economic system. This can result in the conversion of many smaller groups into the values and mores of the political power that has taken over.

Although prejudice may continue based on ethnicity or class, the culture of the dominant group or majority can merge, must merge, with the others, into the greater national whole, with minorities eventually losing distinctiveness. Very strong partisans, however, can hold off or attack the dominant group or split into rebellious and critical factions. Historical and social accounts from one side or the other should be treated with suspicion. Two or three different overlapping rather than antagonistic accounts would offer majority/minority insights not provided by the dominant group alone.

b. Ethnocentric and Narcissistic

Ethnocentrism is found in all societies, and may be defined as a deep-seated feeling that one's own society is normal and superior to others. It is not only a case of "we are the greatest" but also a feeling that "our" standards and values are normal. This implies that other peoples are abnormal, primitive, less developed, and rather odd. We feel right and the righter we feel the more we see others as strange and primitive, when that is simply the way their culture developed.

"Centric" attitudes also ally with a sense of self that is comfortable with superiority, and a tendency to view everyone and everything through this one set of lenses, "we're the best," "the greatest," the most civilized and intelligent, and so on. These lenses may be rose-colored for the insiders, and quite different shades for others. Within the relatively open society that is America, women are still a small part of the story which is centered on male heroes for the most part.[20]

After all, ethnocentrism is viewing others through the eyes of only one's own culture without switching lenses or putting feet in others' shoes. This provides the viewer with a wonderfully narrow and self-satisfied view of other histories and traditions distorted by what should be the values "we" hold. We are adopting and exporting our own propaganda in this story, and most of this is unlikely to be appreciated in other places, cultures, and nations.

The problem for teaching history in any nation or culture is that ethnocentric views may be quite wrong in their views of others, resulting in dangerous misinterpretations and abuses of the "foreign" people and their idea and beliefs. Seeing ourselves as civilized and others as savages yields a very distorted historical narrative, but tells a great deal about how we view ourselves. Ethnocentric attitudes are not very useful ways of analyzing or interpreting history, much less teaching the subject, but prejudice and distortion do make a great lesson for discussion.

Worse yet, the only rosy views of one's own culture may also misinterpret and justify the actions of "our" current government officials in dealing with "foreign" peoples and nations, many of whom have joined us and become citizens. Ethnocentrism is a kind of blindness to the values of others, to their physical state of being, to their lives as human beings, however different or alike they are to and from "us." In many cases, prejudice and bias can actually cloud historical judgment to such an extent that we lack all understanding of people, places, and events and wind up making some very costly mistakes about who we attack and/or try to save in places where "we" don't really understand the cultures and their own local conflicts.

c. Philosophical: Superiority/Inferiority Complex

Perhaps the most extensive and harmful views derive from or express the sense that "others" are subhuman and animal-like, and can be dealt with in much the way livestock or vermin are treated. A sense of superiority over all others is a first assumption of sweeping prejudice that puts the bearer at the top of the mountain, and almost all others below. Social studies classrooms may be able to help create a sense of global and national belonging by rewriting textbooks to give more and better attention to race and gender as well as treat other issues.[21]

In some cases, "civilized" peoples (self-described) may commit the most savage attacks on uncivilized peoples, usually peoples of color and/or of lower technological development. The leadership then turns it around to blame the attacked for their incivility and lack of thanks for what amounts to an invasion and colonization of their territory.

Prejudice against other people as less than human can result in tragic outcomes both for them, conquerors and conquered, leading to ruin for one or both. Many nations and empires have successfully survived and prospered by convincing the conquered (if alive) that the masters and their culture and government are the height of civilization. Philosophy and economics have been utilized to promote socialization of peoples and have absorbed many cultures. Cultural conquest may be viewed as beneficent compared to those who feel the inferior should be exiled or exterminated.

Bias pervades historical thinking and action, including the present, and must be guarded against in drawing quick and easy conclusion about which people, places, and events have been included or excluded from the narrative, any narrative.

KEY QUESTIONS TO CONSIDER, APPLY, AND EVOLVE

- What are some of the main motivations behind bias?
- Is bias usually hidden or open in historical writing?
- Can news be biased, and can there be news without views?
- Is bias usually based on social values, or arises from personal prejudice, or both, or neither?
- How can we as teachers and students guard against bias? Give a few examples.
- How can we control or at least raise awareness of our own biases?
- Is bias the same as prejudice, ethnocentrism, superiority, or closed-mindedness? Why or why not?
- To deny that we are one species, all human, is to see history as a constant conquest of the undeserving and primitive: agreed or disagreed?

NOTES

1. Allport, G. (1979). *The Nature of Prejudice*. New York: Perseus Books.
2. Anderson, Benedict (1983). *Imagined Communities: Reflections on the Origin and Spread of Nationalism*. London: Verso.
3. Gioseffi, D. (ed.) (1993). *On Prejudice: A Global Perspective*. New York: Anchor Books.
4. Hobsbawm, Eric J. (1992). *Nations and Nationalism since 1780: Programme, Myth, Reality* (2nd ed.). Cambridge: Cambridge University Press.
5. Kinder, Donald R., and Kam, Cindy D. (2009). *Us Against Them: Ethnocentric Foundations of American Opinion*. Chicago: University of Chicago Press.
6. Feagin, J. R. (2006). *Systemic Racism: A Theory of Oppression*. New York: Routledge.
7. Graves, Joseph. (2004). *The Race Myth*. NY: Dutton.
8. Marcellinus, A. (1939). *The Roman History*. Loeb Classical Library (Vol. III) 2. Harvard University, 383–391.

9. Hammond, R. A., and Axelrod, R. (2006). "The evolution of ethnocentrism" *Journal of Conflict Resolution* 50(6), 926–936.

10. Smith, Anthony D. (2010) [2001]. *Nationalism: Theory, Ideology, History* (2nd ed.). Cambridge University: Polity Press.

11. Hobsbawm, Eric J. (1992). *Nations and Nationalism Since 1780: Programme, Myth, Reality* (2nd ed.). Cambridge: Cambridge University Press.

12. Allen, Theodore. (1994). *The Invention of the White Race, Volume 1*. London: Verso.

13. Allen, Theodore. (1997). *The Invention of the White Race, Volume 2*. London: Verso.

14. Bonilla-Silva, Eduardo (2018). *Racism without Racists: Color-Blind Racism and the Persistence of Racial Inequality in the United States*. Rowman & Littlefield Publishers, Inc.

15. Brugar, K., Halvorsen, A.-L., Hernandez, S. (January/February, 2014). "Where are the women? A classroom inquiry into Social studies textbooks" *NCSS: Social Studies and the Young Learner* 3, 28–31.

16. Collins, G. (2003). *America's Women: 400 Years of Dolls, Drudges, Helpmates, and Heroines*. New York: HarperCollins.

17. Lerner, Gerda (1986). *Women and History, Part I, The Creation of Patriarchy*. New York: Oxford University Press, 8–10.

18. Blumberg, R. L. (2008). *Gender Bias in Textbooks; Hidden Obstacle on the Road to Gender Equality in Education* (2008/ED/EFA/MRT/PI/18) New York: UNESCO, 1–54.

19. Photograph of a common quarter, 7 October 2019 by author.

20. Frederickson, M. (2004). "Surveying gender: Another look at the way we teach United States history" *The History Teacher* 37(4), 476–484.

21. Harriman, H. (1997). "Women's history and the National Standards for world history: Change and continuity" *Journal of Women's History* 9(3), 161–163.

Chapter 4

Story

Fact and Fiction and in Between

What is at issue here is not: What are the facts? but rather: How are the facts to be described in order to sanction one mode of explaining them rather than another? Some historians will insist that history cannot become a science until it finds the technical terminology adequate to the correct characterization of its objects of study, in the way that physics did in the calculus and chemistry did in the periodic tables. Others will continue to insist that the integrity of historiography depends on its use of ordinary language, its avoidance of jargon.[1]

OVERVIEW

Story and storylines are the main topic in this chapter and are deeply embedded features in most human communications, fact or fiction. History as story, claiming a factual basis, may have more in common with literature than science, setting up a deep conflict in how to relate the past to the present.

HEADLINE!

Television and the Internet make it easier than ever to broadcast what we say to untold millions, billions, and given that so much of what we say is false and deceptive, no doubt whatever lies we tell fall on unprecedented numbers of innocent ears.

Figure 4.1 The Capitoline She-Wolf[2] Mother of twin suckling infants Romulus and Remus founders of Rome A story: Romulus and Remus suckling Mother's milk before growing up to found Rome. Source: Original in Rome/image in the public domain presented on Wikipedia Commons.

I. STORY VARIETIES/NARRATIVES/DOCUMENTS

Story, central to both history and literature, has many meanings, many styles, many goals. Tales that are invented and tales that are true can be presented in exactly the same way, and that's a problem for all of us to play with, from fairy tales to truth to fake news.[3]

A story can range across the historical sense of chronological development with an explanation of causes from precise public records to tall tales about the biggest fish you ever caught. Storytellers are still very much valued in society over thousands of years. Their roles as entertainers abound not only in history, but also in many media, filmed, sung, written, and texted. Often the line between fact and fiction is hard to discern, and sometimes it is purposely and totally blurred by the author or creator. In some cases, political leaders can take up the story form and be quite inventive with it.

For teaching and learning social science and history, story as a concept can be thought of in at least four useful ways: literature, journalism, testimony, and historical narrative. All are narratives in some way but some aim at reporting or telling about real events, while others are rewarded for the inventiveness of the tale, its characters, plot, and outcome. Thinking about history as mixing purposes and genres can help you to develop great questions about the real or imagined or mix documentary you are offering to the class.

a. Literary

Literature is inventive writing from an author's imagination. The creator writes the tale, and offers a plot, action, characters, and language, beautiful seductive language, if possible. This use of language turns a story into an art form that we all love to read and discuss.

Stories are of course invented but bear some semblance, purposely or inadvertently, to real life. Symbols of old are employed to make a point and increase sales, like *Game of Thrones*. Characters are described and played in ways that draw the viewer in and produce both interest and affection. In many ways, an author's characters express views that reflect a past time and place, but also seep into the present in the manner issues are presented and decisions made. Some focus on love, others on power, but most are mix of many emotions and decisions.

The deliberate use of language and imagery, or sound, to impress and entice the reader or viewer is characteristic of fictional literature. Social scientists and historians must be competent and clear, but are not expected to produce literary masterpieces though many try. The professional end all and be all of history is an *accurate portrayal* of past times, places, people, and events. The end all and be all of literature is to draw folks into the story and its characters as they move through an exciting plot to a hopefully satisfying conclusion.

End all and be all, however, yields forms of crossover literature, historical fiction, doctored documentaries, stories that are part fact and part fancy. This genre mix is great for teachers who want to engage student learning and ask a lot of provocative questions that hopefully will build understanding and insight.[4] We all love a good story!

b. Journalist

Much of what we read is reported by journalists who usually represent newspapers, publishers, or government services. The art of reporting has been honed over several centuries at least. Journalism has roots in historical narratives, with the difference being that journalism dates from the advent of printing on a mass scale around the sixteenth century in Europe and China.[5]

Journalists used historical reports, chronicles, written notices, and broadsheets to present "news" of the sixteenth to nineteenth centuries often illustrated with woodcuts and etchings. The style of writing tended to be more factual and direct than literature, and focused on relating newsworthy events. All of journalism, so called, is of great historical value much like diaries and travelogues, but more pointed toward current events.

Most journalism would fall into the history/social science category, fact driven, but might be used for taking sides in a dispute or staking out a political position. For example, a most famous bit of journalism, Thomas Paine's *Common Sense*, bolstered the American Revolution by distributing 100,000 copies in the colonies, a huge printing for the time. This was journalism that was part of and also made history. And it was well written to boot.

Journalists follow very historian-like codes of ethics stressing the sources they used in reporting, separating fact and opinion, where possible, and trying to be present at an event. There are many codes available to look at but there are certain common agreements. These include one or more of the following:

1. Journalists should be at an event they are reporting on or have a number of credible and reliable eyewitnesses to draw upon.
2. Journalists should try to report objectively remaining neutral in disputes between and among peoples and nations.
3. Journalists should weigh stories in terms of justifiable consequences, that is, balance news against potentially harmful consequences to participants and bystanders.
4. Journalist should maintain a commitment to the world community and report accurately without bending to the local or national loyalties.
5. Journalists should make their judgments and positions clear to readers, separating editorial remarks from reporting the news.[6]

Thus, journalism is much like writing narrative history, often in a more direct, user-friendly style, though there is a range of literary levels in both history and journalism, around the world. A story is usually told chronologically with quotes from witnesses and the journalistic does not editorialize more than a bit. Editorials, that is opinions and judgments, are fine but should be identified as such, hence the creation of an "op-ed" page where editors and readers give and defend opinions and explain viewpoints.[7] The growing problem of so-called fake news is not at all new to history or journalism. There has been fake news around since writing began, but that gives us great opportunities to teach how to recognize, research, and combat fake news in the search for trustworthy and reliable information. A recent headline in the *New York Times* exemplifies trends by declaring that, "Americans Trust Local News: That Belief Is Being Exploited." The article goes on to say, "As consumers become more skeptical about the national news they encounter online, impostor local sites that promote ideological agendas are becoming more common."[8] In earlier times, there may

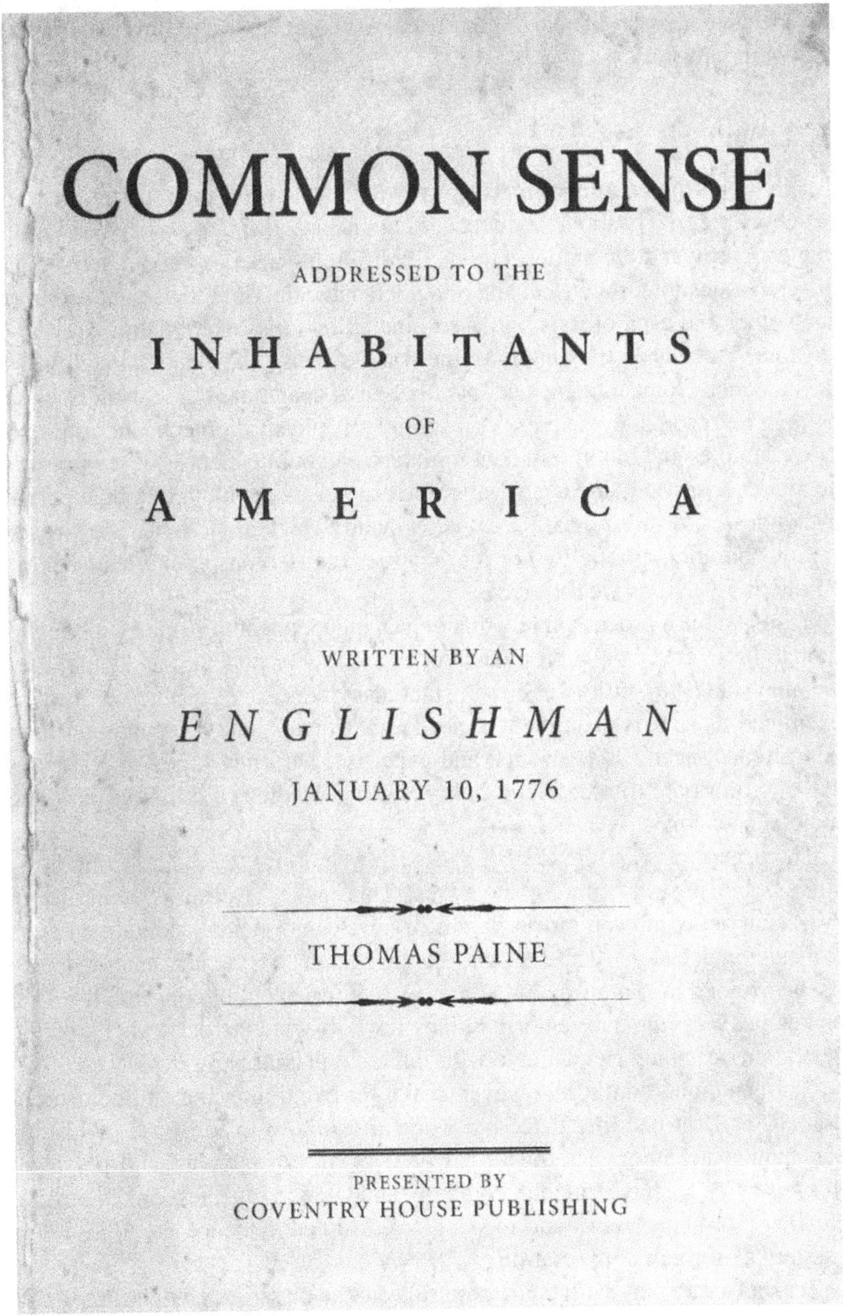

COMMON SENSE

ADDRESSED TO THE

INHABITANTS

OF

AMERICA

WRITTEN BY AN

ENGLISHMAN

JANUARY 10, 1776

THOMAS PAINE

PRESENTED BY
COVENTRY HOUSE PUBLISHING

Figure 4.2 Facsimile of *Common Sense* by Thomas Paine, 1776. Source: Library of Congress Public Domain, Washington, DC.

have been similar problems, but there was a lot less news and fewer sources to deal with in history.[9]

c. Testimony

Testimony is the relating of facts by eyewitnesses, experts, and participants in whatever the trial is about. Evidence, as in history, also plays a key role. Both the testimony and the evidence come in different varieties and are subject to different questions. Accusers and defenders have the right to ask questions of each other and each other's witnesses, including cross-examination.

Much depends on the quality of the witnesses, and the extent and nature of the evidence. Some evidence counts for a great deal more than others, such as cell phone records, eyewitness corroborations, physical objects and artifacts, DNA samples and blood tests, photographs, and public records. Eyewitnesses are direct observers, and usually regarded as most valuable, more than partial eyewitnesses, or those nearby, or secondhand, which are less well-regarded.

Corroboration among two or more parties on accounts strengthens a case, conflicting versions weaken a case.

Testifying is a process in law that values independent third-party witnesses though these are not always available, and if few or none are available, then we may have to settle for circumstantial evidence.[10, 11] Witnesses can be examined and cross-examined as needed but their quality depends on their competence, nearness to events, and expertise. Different kinds of witnesses can all contribute to a case and help resolve it leading to a unified jury and judicial decision.

There may also be areas of inconsistency, missing evidence, conflicting stories, and hostility among witnesses. This makes a case a lot harder to prosecute or defend and much like history, we can only make tentative or circumstantial decisions. The case may be "hung," that is, the jury cannot decide or is corrupted in some way, or a case can be thrown out of court totally. That makes lawyers unhappy and historians have to work harder to achieve the best inferences they can achieve with limited and confusing evidence.

Confusion and conflict, however, make for exciting crime and courtroom dramas, and for exciting detective work in trying to make sense of history and human behavior. The historical process, historiography, and the legal rules of evidence have much in common, and yield many questions to pursue. However, clashing views and missing or corrupted evidence often promotes exciting classroom conversations.

Teachers may play with courtroom rules in the classroom by putting someone famous on trial, like trying King Louis XVI for negligence in bringing on the French Revolution. Newspaper accounts and political blogs can also be tested and weighed, focusing on "real news vs. fake news," for example.[12] Play court of last resort as both drama and history.

d. History/Social Science

Historical method aims at creating truthful accounts of the past based on credible eyewitnesses and reports. No fake news, please, and sources duly noted, thanks.

Texts should be believable, consistent, and reliable. Best if these are corroborated by other texts. Best if the author is straightforward and open-minded, rather than full of biased opinions and personal prejudices. But, authorship, artistry, and other media may also serve as the basis for drawing conclusions about a past time and place or another place in the world.[13]

Best if the source is authentic, meaning of the time and place of which she/he writes. Wonderful if you have a real text of the time that is not corrupted by other commentary and/or copied over (several times?) or missing pieces filled in. Superior documents offer commentary from several witnesses and several sides, including maybe outside observers giving testimony.

If the historian writing the history has a clear outlook, an overall philosophy, and belongs to a narrative tradition and viewpoint, that is all to the good. The readers or teachers or students have a good fix on where the author is "coming from" in terms of her/his approach to past and present people and events.[14] Thus, contrary to many teachers' views, if the historian makes clear what theory or model they are following, better guidance for thinking develops. For example, two different theories can be juxtaposed to bolster discussion, for example, Carlyle (great people make history), or Marx (social movements make history) proposed as two models.[15]

Historical theory can guide applications, like the Annales school (big history that includes technology and art and ordinary people), or a social history approach (working people and places, social change). We can research those methods and applications to increase our understanding of the evidence, and learn how the historians of each approach developed interpretations and reached conclusions on causes and effects.

We will also have a better grasp of the process by which value judgments were arrived at as well. Of course, just as the law wants solid witnesses, so too does history want abundant and solid evidence. Alas, like law courts, history suffers from many deficiencies. Eyewitnesses can be a very mixed bag of liars, incompetents, and suffer from poor memories or planned loss, be self-interested, and venal.

There may be conflicts among witnesses and also reporters and historians, with different accounts offered and no resolution in sight. Ideologies may be hidden from the reader, to appear later upon a realization that the source is biased or politically motivated. Authors may suffer from values that are racist, sexist, and ethnocentric. Their testimony may need close analysis and questioning.

All evidence has to be reviewed and reevaluated, causing a revision in conclusions, or no conclusion at all.

For teachers and students, all of these problems make for a very exciting court case, mystery, and historical narrative full of issues to discuss and problems to examine and solve.[16] Boredom fades away in much the same way as when watching a tense and complex mystery where the outcome is uncertain and the murderer unidentified. Issues with evidence gives us an historiographical run for the money and we get to test the rules as we go deeper into the story.

II. STRUCTURE AND GENRE

Story is a concept that we use to relate people, places, and events to each other. The tale well-told is an ancient device, probably prehistoric, that is still employed by almost anyone trying to talk to a spouse or child, or sell to Hollywood. Stories can be personal, professional, and institutional. As an amateur historian, you might draw up a family story or prepare a memoir.[17]

As a professional, you would collect sources, analyze and compare, test and criticize, and eventually produce an organized narrative. You might use artsy metaphorical language or ordinary descriptive language. How you use language will impact the account strongly. Remember, in social science and history, just as in literature and the arts, a good story sells well.

And as in a story, the tale follows a long-honored list of rules for writing a true story or an invented story. A mythical story may have the same structure as a historical narrative, and use similar literary devices. For example, the story may fall into a specific category of written expression, for example, memoir, biography, satire, description, essay, mystery, science fiction, horror, romance, and journalism. There are many more categories and subcategories, but the differences may be minor.

The point is that writers and historians all use the same styles and genres, with a narrative structure of some kind, a plan of action, plot and characters, as well as a mood and attitude governed by an overall philosophy.

a. Genre: Real and Imagined

Genres were invented to tell tales and produce narratives and each has its own focus and rules. There is an imaginary dividing line between fact and fiction, particularly in history, with labels like folktale, fable, historical fiction, documentary, autobiography, and most recently narrative nonfiction.

While historical narrative aims at factual reporting, and historical fiction uses and abuses facts to novelize a story and imagine what's missing, narrative nonfiction seeks a middle ground where a true event is given a stylish treatment using the tools of more creative literature. Nonfiction implies we are reading a true story, fiction implies that we are reading an invention.

Herein lies one of the great dangers of history, and the great advantages of storytelling.

History is replete with stories, and often follows chronological story form, mostly from past to present, but sometimes in the present and going backward. The danger is that the better the storytelling, the more believable it becomes and the more rapt the reader, who eventually suspends all suspicions and is swept away by a tale well told in lovely language. Believable language, skillful language.[18] The problem is that readers think not of reality but of the beautiful literary creation of the history writer, and can scarcely divide fact from fiction.

Language can be seductive, and shapes our affections as well as communicating knowledge. In one historian's or journalist's report and narrative, Napoleon can be the most fascinating person, a great leader and lawgiver, and in another Napoleon can be likened to a tyrant and conqueror, a radical revolutionary and despot, all rolled into one.

Well, if you forget to be SUSPICIOUS! You will accept the best story you read as true! So, whatever the label, keep a critical eye open to the genre and decide if the author has turned King Henry VIII or whoever into a romance, a biography, or a fantasy, or all in one. A great activity would be to ask the students to tell a story of their own, in conversational narrative, from memory alone, as required by the popular radio show, "The Moth."[19]

In a way, fiction, labeled as such, is probably safer to read than a historical narrative using devices borrowed from fiction to tell a story. After a while, genre categories begin to collapse, and you have a big problem with interpretation of evidence. And that problem is exactly what makes teaching history and literature so much fun.

b. Structure and Flow

Each story, true or partly true, or invented (note: I did not say false), has a structure and flow.

Most common for a tale is a linear path where the author or historian follows a straight line in time from birth to death, from the beginning of a war to its end, from a romantic courtship to marriage and family, and so on. The same may be said of many novels as well, although in modern times there is more experimentation with timelines, flashbacks, multiple accounts, invoking the need to discuss "unreliable narrators" as opposed to outright liars.

Linearity has the advantage of making causes and consequences fairly clear. Even flashbacks can be linear as they fit into a chronological story.

There may also be alternative approaches using nonlinear narratives in which multiple characters or speakers provide different accounts of the same events, and switch around out of order. There are many stories, often from diverse viewpoints, some agreeable, some disagreeable, some just plain confusing and purposely perplexing. Some jump through times, backward and forward, some predict the future in a science fiction way, and others move through portals of different times and places to round out a narrative.

Furthermore, there are interactive narratives that invite readers to join in creating characters and moving them across a plot to a desired objective, as satisfying ending to the tale. Narratives have a need to begin with a topic, and develop characters who work to solve certain problems and make policies that result in a resolution, or conclusion, satisfying or not, like getting married, ending a war, spreading an invention, establishing a government, and so on.

This is the narrative structure, usually in four or five parts:

1. Beginning with a problem or issue,
2. Introducing a set of characters, or players,
3. Setting a crisis or turn of events that demand a solution,
4. Moving everyone and the story along in a series of twist and turns of events, and
5. Resolution, or denouement, of the story into a happy, mixed, or sad ending in which we can feel success or failure, and experience an emotional catharsis.[20]

As you can see this is a pretty standard flow of events, and a somewhat boring pattern, but historians, writers, and film producers can play around with all elements to mystify and confuse, entice and enthrall, their reader/viewers. A story may begin with the ending, or open with conflicting accounts, or do a series of flashbacks.

Flow can be shaped, strained to a trickle, burst into a flood of evidence, and play tricks with facts, all to tell a better story. Many historical stories are reported in ways that make them seem very much a good story, and the question is what is real and what is borrowed from literary forms? That's what makes a story interesting and attracts attention.

c. Plot and Action

Just as the flow can be shaped, each and every story needs some sort of plot to carry the narrative forward and backward, and actions to elicit interest.

Figure 4.3 Empress Cixi in Royal Court at Beijing, Circa 1900. Source: Yu Xunling, photographer, Smithsonian Institution, licensed for public domain to Wikipedia. The Empress Cixi in royal court with her full title in Chinese above her plus many symbols and signs of status and prosperity. Think of questions you would like to ask! The Empress Cixi (Yu Xunling, photographer, 1900, Smithsonian Institution. In the public domain in country of origin and other countries, Wikipedia Commons.

Stories can vary greatly in plot, and even more so in action, with some stories being reflective and self-reflective, thinking about and discussing ideas and feelings leading to a decision, like marriage and divorce, while other stories are plot-driven with fast action, conflict all the way along, like a thriller.

A plot is literally the series of events happening to and experienced by characters in the drama of history, in effect a timeline of events. The first and the last Dowager Empress of China, Cixi (ruled 1861–1908) is part of a story in which she acquires power, develops stratagems to hold off foreign powers from slicing up her nation, while still remaining the absolute monarch of a huge empire that desperately needs leadership and modernization.

The tension between tradition and change drives the plot which takes thrilling twists and turns and characters exhibit a log of biases, some quite noble, others quite nasty. Actions include government proclamations, plus a wild uprising of anti-imperialist Chinese people called "the Boxers" (1899–1901) foreign influence, territorial grabs, lying and cheating, clueless bureaucrats, spying and intrigue, personality clashes, pomp and circumstance, and the beginnings of a vast revolution for China.

Each action drives the plot forward as we breathlessly await success or failure at modernization and change while an old empress of traditional ancestry and royal blood tries to stem the destruction and dismantling of her nation. This true history has the making of a great story with a gripping plot and lots of intrigue and violence. Do you really care if the story is true or not? Is the plot uplifting or depressing, and how do we decide on the value of the story and its players for drawing many historical insights and conclusions.

d. Characters

Characters are the people who live in a story. They may be real in a history account, or through their own writing; or they may be fictitious, invented by an author and wholly or partly invented. The characters that populate a story give a human quality and invite involvement. History and literature lovers should keep in mind that much the same language is used in much the same way to describe fictional and real people. This is a limitation of language but also provides a richness of observation and description often lacking in official documents.

We like our fiction and our history dressed up in evocative language, and that helps us to visualize the past and the future.[21] Textbooks are often dry and pedantic, traveling through a story as though it was a shopping list. We usually have no real investment or empathy for the characters. Sometimes we don't even have a decent insight into the character's motivations or their cultural values. This lack of insight is all the more to be pitied since it not only dulls the tale, but it prevents us from caring about people and events.

Characters allow us to identify with people both like and unlike ourselves, but enough like us so we can build empathy for their plight in the story. Empathy, for example, for characters in *Game of Thrones*, an intensely popular historical fantasy, creates interest and broadens our grasp of unstable historical political situations, that is, warring kingdoms. Upon careful examination, the story is almost completely modeled on English medieval history and horror fables from the British Isles and Scandinavia. Almost all literature is, after all, based on reality, although once in a while history imitates fiction.

We tend to relate to characters when they share their hopes and dreams, inner psychology, and crises or successes with us in a story. As in fiction, so in history, the closer we get to a character, even one we don't particularly like, the more attention we pay to their role in the plot, or action. In the hands of a good historian or historical fiction writer characters can be "brought to life," using sources and even better, their own writings from their time and place.

How evidence is selected for a character will greatly shape your judgment of their personality. Autobiographies help in formulating a historical personality or a fictional one, too. Character formation and understanding is a complex and difficult exercise and may or may not result in a convincing character. Usually, we know bits and pieces of a character slowly fleshing out a full-fledged personality.

In many stories and histories, characters, especially political, actually tend to fall into a pattern that is heroic or evil, with the "real" figure hard to discern. The story becomes one of heroism and a journey, injustice and rebellion, love and crises, persecution and flight, anger and murder. Characters may be typecast and misinterpreted using literary similes and metaphors.

Other, "social" histories, focus more on common people or rebels or inventors or artists, but even here there is the tendency to judge and categorize. It takes a great deal of study and reflection to grasp a character's role and meaning, if fictional, their career and actions, if a real figure in history. Either way, one must be careful and *suspicious*! of jumping to conclusions about a character's actions and motivation, and their place in history.

The urge to moralize about characters wells up from deep within us, so watch out!

III. OVERALL JUDGMENT OF STORIES/HISTORIES/ HERSTORIES: ATTITUDE AND VALUES

History and story share a sense of emotion and judgment that arise from the human condition that values sympathy, empathy and moral judgment, or outrage and condemnation.

Though many social scientists and historians have fought over the idea of ethical or moral judgment of past times, leaders, and practices, it seems almost inevitable and uncontrollable.[22] Better to admit up-front one's philosophy and value system or one's attempt to maintain a fair and open objectivity than to have it leak out over many areas of a narrative. It is particularly important to identify evaluations of characters' actions, and demonstrate the base of support for the historical or literary judgment.

Authors, whether songwriters, novelists, or social scientists and historians follow their research from facts to interpretation and then on to some sort of judgment, over or covert, that informs the overall outcome. As the story develops in plot, characters, and actions, attitudes come out from hiding, language conveying a sense of judgment about good or bad decisions, ending perhaps with a moral or ethical stand. Online reports on the Internet have the same or worse problems of judgment and attitude as traditional format presentations and extend to vital parts of history like the cold war, maybe all wars.[23]

Language appears with "hot" words or "cold" words that describe characters, who slowly become more heroic or more villainous, better or worse decision-makers. As the plot progresses and more actions are taken, or not taken, stronger identities develop and begin to like various characters or despise others, rightly or wrongly.

This is the point in our inquiry where we have to arouse our suspicions about building too much sympathy or hatred for a character, and start analyzing what they actually did in history or in the plot of the novel. Conclusions can begin with straightforward description of events, then move into symbolism and signals, yielding new insights through literary and historical analysis.

a. Straightforward to Symbolic

Begin to develop "feelings" for various characters, positive and negative as well as in-between. Feelings can arise in a historical study as of an autobiography, a novel as much as a journal report. A story can deeply affect our emotions, and shift our judgment of a character dramatically. Current political figures inspire these kinds of shits, and can command great affection and sympathy.

Keep a diary of your feelings and evaluations of characters, perhaps matching one from a historical novel to one from an historians' study of a real person. Or use a TV historical drama matched to an historian's account. Note which events and actions influence how you feel, and then rethink it all at the conclusion of your study. Choose a character with heroic qualities and with flaws. Don't romanticize them at all, if possible.

We tend to abandon stories that are confusing or dull, without affect.

At first, the story seems straightforward, moving on chronologically and without ethical implications. Then actions and decisions are related that change our views of the players, with some drawing our disapproval, others our admiration. Actions bring us closer to the characters and the plot. We decide that some are worthy of our affections, while we reconsider others.

Symbols come into play (sometimes many and meaningful, other times few). As we rethink and review the story's seemingly simple actions, we begin to notice changes, and these can be subtle or obvious. There may be key turning points, like the Boxer Rebellion in the story of the Dowager Empress of China. The story may contain humor, charm, success, depression, failure, and extinction. Signs are given early on that the plot will be fun or tragic.

The opening sentences or scene foretell the shape of things to come. In teaching English, we have encountered a topic sentence setting the tone, language, and evolution of a story. We might invent a "topic" sentence that draws the reader or viewer into the tale. For example, opening the film *Elizabeth* (1998, UK, Shekhar Kapur, director) with a scene of people burning at the stake for their faith sets a tone of despair and conflict immediately.

As historians/social scientists, we begin to ask questions: who is being burned, and why? And by whom is the fire being lit? who gave the order? What sort of language is used to describe people and events? Does language rich in adjectives and emotional words influence us in our views of historical personalities as the story progresses? Are we aware of the way language and images shape our judgments, and can we resist being railroaded into a positive or negative view rather than a balanced assessment of accomplishments?

Moving into bigger historical questions about how and why a story is presented helps us think about the reasons behind action, and authorship. We begin to see language as both communication and seduction, and what is the symbolism of the stake, of fire, or faith?

Stories rise from history, from tales to be told, accounts to be settled, emotions expressed, and new ideas to be communicated.

b. Believability and Agenda

The story may be so powerful and intriguing that we are quickly caught up in the plot, and begin caring what happens to the characters. Real and/or fictional characters develop depth and become "believable," meaning that we are ready to lend credence to them as part of the action. As we gain a better grasp of a story, its chronology and the culture from which it springs, we raise new questions about believability for both real history and fiction.

Checking facts and other sources, especially competing sources, becomes more important to corroborate a story with other stories. Do they match? How different or similar are the stories to each other? Comparisons and expansion of textual and visual sources provides a sharper grasp of events and raise questions of hidden values within documents, texts, and literature.

Realization develops that our sources, whether art, music, literature, or documents, was written by someone with beliefs, values, and interpretations. The story, however fantastic or allegorical, is trying to communicate an idea that includes (probably) judgments about history an author wants us to accept and believe. Historians, even superb scholars, delve deep into the lives of their subjects and may come to admire them all the more, or despise them, whatever their faults.

Reading two or more biographers of a president, for example, Lyndon Johnson, may result in almost opposite evaluations, leaving the reader to figure out what were the authors' "hidden agendas" of values. Did the values come with the author and shape the story or did the study for the story shape the agenda? Identifying an author's or artists' ideological views, and value judgments offers clues to the way they report the story, and the history.

Values can be vitally important to how we see a person or event in history, or why we forget whole swaths of story and concentrate only on narrow sections of the big picture. For example, there is a very strong readership for war history and especially for Americans, Civil War history. And historians respond by producing ever more and ever more varied views of the history of battles for us to consider.[24]

Yet, other portions of the story are relatively ignored, laying there on the bookshelves or art libraries underappreciated, like the 1850s leading up the Civil War, or the Jim Crow era after the collapse of Reconstruction. War is exciting and resolvable, and usually there's a winner, but in social history, cycles roll over and over again, with solutions often stuck or ricocheting between different agendas. Sometimes one agenda takes hold and becomes dominant, Civil Rights, Robber Barons, the Great Depression, overlooking social failures to integrate, demands for more equality, social dislocation, and poverty, for instance.

As believability takes hold we may care for one side or another in a social dispute, revolutionary movement, suffrage campaign, or conflict. Our reactions well up from our own personality, politics, and background, but also from our manipulation by the author, artist, or composer of the storyline. As sympathies arise in us, we are in greater danger of arousing suspicions that we too have adopted one agenda and overlooked others before coming to a reasoned judgment of a period of history and its denizens. Or, we may be horrified or tired of the entire event and its players, wishing to leave, like getting stuck in a foxhole or trench in the middle of World War I.

Events may take on a sense of awe, a sense of support for, or antagonism toward, many of the characters in the story, or the history. A story may grip us so strongly that its believability is nearly total, or we reject it out of hand as fantasy. Yet, a more balanced inquiry may lend some credence to both sides in a disputed or contested history that has to be carefully adjudicated and refined. Belief is not necessarily truth. Nor is fiction lacking in facts.

Therefore, storylines can inspire belief, but overlook agenda, agency, and truth, whereas we need close attention to how and why we have decided to take a tale to heart and adopt it.

c. Perplexity versus Interpretation and "the moral of the story"

Dealing with historical events is complex and requires acts of imagination and inference. In attempting to return to the past, much less go back to the future, a reconstruction must create not only the artifacts of a time, but its language and symbols, its values and mores. Missing portions of a story, real or imagined, cause perplexity that needs to be filled in by research, and through interpolation from available data. Portions that are confusing and open to multiple interpretations need review and comparison.[25]

Different lenses may be offered for viewing a story, through different eyes and from professional scientists and historians.

As teachers and students move through careful analysis of a story, many problems will have to be faced up to in reading the text, viewing images, and recreating sounds and lifestyles. We must project ourselves back in time, but in our minds rather than sitting in a lovely upholstered *Time Machine* (film, 1960), conceived and written by H. G. Wells in 1895. We have to do the hard work of making sense of the story, and should identify, not overlook, perplexing bits and pieces, odd characters, too smooth or too choppy plots. From a historical perspective, the novel can be viewed as part of a wave of scientific speculations about industrialization and the future of humankind.

In Wells' novel, the author provides you with the moral of the story by wrapping it up with an ending that needs critical attention. Newer versions like "Back to the Future" also end up with a message and a moral about going back and coming forward. Both author and director are messaging us with philosophical ideas inviting us to consider history as science fiction, and science fiction as history. The whole concept of time travel is part of history, and where we land is open to question.

A moral, or judgment, a happy or sad ending, is the author's choice or history's choice. The ending may be concocted to provide a point, a message, as a finale that gives us a sense of satisfaction and closure. In history and in story, we want the good to triumph (usually) and the evil to be defeated and disappear. We want a story with a happy ending, or at least a hopeful ending.

We hope for a moral that offers philosophical insight and advice in dealing with events and people: a moral that is part of a higher value system based on creed, ideology, or religion. Or, an author might suggest a new value for us to mull over, altruism, activism, revolution, withdrawal.

Usually endings are stereotypical in literature, but in history events are a lot harder to reduce to a simple judgment about good and evil. A range of motives and values, ideologies and religions begin to take shape as influences on our lives, past lives, and presumably future lives. A good story or history account deepens insight into personality and historical behaviors.

People are a very mixed bag of motives and ideas, often acting at variance with their own stated objectives much less in the name of an ideology or faith.

Thus, after students and teachers have discussed, not accepted, the moral of a story, they also need to come up with an ethical view of their own, defended by reason and evidence. This is no easy task if you want a solid moral or judgment based on fact not simply opinion, and requires deep analysis of historical documents and philosophies. Rarely happens.

But, bit by bit, we can creep toward a more nuanced, reasoned judgment about cause and effect, good and evil that is not based in a simple Manicheanism, divided sharply between dark forces and light forces. Darth Vader, in the script of *Star Wars*, was after all, a fallen angel and a light saber alone was not enough to defeat him in *Star Wars*.

IV. DEVELOPING MULTIPLE NARRATIVES AND LEARNING FROM ALL

a. Multiple Narratives

Most teachers and students have never experienced real history: only managed cookie-cutter history nicely arranged and edited for them.

Stories are recounted, swallowed, and repeated, but rarely questioned. Some are quickly forgotten. Others are never approached or given much respect.

Teachers mean well, but conform to the going curriculum, going documentary choices, going popular methods, going lists of goals, objectives, and lists and lists and lists of "facts, facts, facts." In reality, most history and the allied social sciences are complex and offer problems of understanding, corroboration, and judgments. Conclusions should be treated as provisional, unless checked against sources, and subject to checking and criticism.

Worse yet, most students and teachers have very little sense of theory, the overall philosophies behind historical inquiry. Therefore, we go one step at a time in a linear fashion, usually chronologically, to a regurgitated conclusion made by someone else. We are not often clear on how we got from facts to conclusions.

Choosing documents, primary, secondary, or tertiary can be a laborious but enjoyable process for teachers and students of history. Documents, widely conceived in all media, from written to media, from artifact to art, should be selected for their impact on learners, providing a sense of drama, mystery, and eternal questions.

Material for the classroom should present problems that draw learners into historical questions, shrewdly introducing evidence that provokes thinking almost immediately, raising multiple questions not only about the document itself, but about the methods historian and social science detectives use to draw conclusions about the collection of data.

Historians and scientists, even the best of professionals, are human, and suffer from the same emotions and limitations of our cultures, necessitating corrections, checking, and verification. The love of a good story grips us in context, even the sciences, with literature and history thriving on story. A time and place, a culture and a political system, often influence our views of historical people and events, causing a paralysis of critical thinking in favor of stereotypical or biased thinking that matches the temper of the times.

Cultural conditions shape views to fit with popular assumptions about the world, why people act, and what language and feelings should be used to describe eras and episodes.

b. Human Emotions and Limitations

Our species is earth conquering and invasive, but has deep roots in social networking. We survive and conquer by social process and uniting together.

Even prehumans, not yet homo sapiens, from hundreds of thousands of years ago, spread across nearly the entire planet limited only by lack of technology to cross wide oceans and dense ice packs. Although controversial, it is hard to imagine they could accomplish migrations without language and leadership and cooperation.

Cooperation within a people, call it a tribe or a nation, produced higher and more coordinated levels of accomplishment, even in the earliest ancient world that are quite astounding: like the Great Wall of China, the Pyramids of Egypt and Central America, or the Roman Roads, but this cooperation also produced internal cultures that created their own views of the world.

Each society developed its own culture, language, and beliefs, to help survive as a group, but so did other groups. As peoples developed and migrated, their cultural differences made them suspicious of others, mistrustful, and sometimes violent. Conflicts arose over differences, territory, trade, and travel that created limitations on cooperation.

Successful societies that mastered increasingly sophisticated technologies tended to swallow up, drive off, or dispose of competing groups, particularly resistant competition. Those that could not or would not adapt quickly to changing conditions often disappeared or were most likely absorbed by the dominant group. Thus, Neanderthal genes survive in many peoples, but not to a great extent. Denisovians, Heidelbergensis, and other early full humans also became minor contributors to the overall gene pool, as far as we know now.

We have given various names to these conflicts, for example, war, skirmish, combat, conquest, each people inventing their own justifications for action, creating limitations on knowing the truth about other peoples, especially the losers. Therefore, throughout history, most certainly since the State was invented, internal groups, tribes, peoples, cultures, nations, have their own stories to tell with their own values and narratives of history. So, be careful about totally accepting any one-side tales.

"Our" narratives may disagree strongly with theirs, other people's narratives, making truth much more difficult to obtain for "them." All sides have stories and those stories can conflict or agree, but almost always yield interesting differences in point of view and style. Now people have the power to change the climate, fish out the oceans, and level mountains, and cross the earth for conquest and control. Yet, tribe and nation, competition and cooperation, still live within us all in our stories of great leaders, conquests, and accomplishments, which value views win and whose views win out really makes a difference. Storytelling may lead to group cohesion, or to a collapse, provide power and economic success, or cut a wide swath of collapse and destruction.

Thus, a major limitation on teaching and learning history is the all too human tendency to identify with "their own" story and view those "outside" as "others" who tell different and untrue stories about us, and themselves. Bias is quite natural and quite dangerous in telling tales of heritage and conquest, perhaps building loyalty but limiting understanding. Alas, in human history, we are widely sharing pretty much the same stories of nationhood and beginnings, of evolution and adventure, not very different overall.

Therefore, giving the "enemy" a break, and listening to their story, or viewing "primitives" or competitors, as people, becomes a challenge to understanding the sequence and scope of history.

Without listening to competing narratives and tales, it is almost impossible to understand one's own culture and history.

c. Storytelling: Originals and Embellishments

Humans love storytelling. Even with the decline of readership (at least on paper) in this, the so-called advanced technological twenty-first century, people gravitate toward stories. They are in fact story freaks," checking the latest tweets, messages, texts, and emails throughout the day, walking while reading, perhaps hitting a lamppost or bumping into a fellow human as they read "viral" films, breaking news, government propaganda, fake news, talk show hosts, blogs, and once in a while, looking at serious historical or social scientific sites.

Storytelling is both pervasive and invasive. We speak the language of stories in everyday speech telling each other tales, and we enjoy listening to or reading or viewing stories in fictional, semi-fictional, and "factual" documentary fashion. In the process of inventing, editing, and embellishing a story, we may create a much better tale than the original, bordering on fiction, or perhaps outright fiction.

We could argue that films, paintings, and novels *from and about* historical events and people provide entertainment, as well as offering some modicum of truth. In some cases, it is wholly entertainment, concocted as they say of "whole cloth" itself an historical expression. But the inventions themselves are history offering hidden agendas, views, images, and emotions that give us evidence of the thinking and times of the producers and consumer.

Language is vitally important to history, as is image and sound, but language is probably most important when we have written records. Management of language becomes an issue in translating and presenting stories and historical documents. A limitation of language is that meaning may shift dramatically or imperceptibly, messages change, and in some cases understanding fails. Languages also communicate a tone or mood in a style and genre that influences emotional reactions by audiences across time and culture.

Storytelling is an art that has been honed as part of human communication perhaps for hundreds of thousands of years, with certain combinations of ideas, characters, and events most pleasing, so pleasing we would like to believe those tales without question. Satisfaction and self-congratulation by a culture are reassuring but hardly help us advance into truthful territory. However, the stories we like in novelistic, historical, or film form yield clues about the time and place we inhabit.

The story of history, like a marriage, tells one or more stories, his-story or her-story, which are often at odds. Folks wind up believing what they most want to believe, and overlooking or rejecting the truth in order to remain satisfied and happy inside the bubble of existence they see as reality. History and stories, when shifting around, undergoing revision, can be quite dangerous, leading to war, revolution, and social condemnation. Whose land was lost? We demand reparations? How have second-class citizens evolved? What can we do about any of these questions without arousing anger and setting off conflict?

Much depends on which stories you believe, and how much you believe them, without getting your historical thinker upper kicking in. Remind yourself of the inherent dangers in acceptance and agreement without checking the sources, and without subjecting stories to criticism from other viewpoints.

We need to hear from those outsiders as well as from insiders we may not like, and throw in few neutral parties as observers, if they can be found.

V. STORYTELLING ACROSS GENRES

Storytelling in the literary sense gives free reign to imagination, character, plot, and action that we welcome as entertainment. So-called historical "fiction" must be based on considerable research but remains free to invent incidents that humanize people and give context to the imagined tales, like film *The Darkest Hour*, about Churchill meeting his public in tube train in London on his way to Parliament. A wonderfully imagined scene of invention and pathos! But was it historical? In character? Likely or unlikely, but something we would love to imagine and believe?

In contrast to the literary premium on imagination and invention, historians and social scientists want very much to describe reality and come to truthful conclusions, even if these are in large part interpretations and narratives based on primary and secondary sources. These also tell stories with plot, characters, and action but are evidence based and footnoted. We can review the author's judgments against a public record of documents and analysis, providing a basis for checking and cross-checking.

History, therefore, holds particular dangers when it ventures into describing topics like character and action, musing about someone's motivations, and telling recounting of wars, elections, and inventions. Political leadership, the role of race, religion, ethnicity, and gender, and the place of "others," can shift in tone and mood to hot emotional subjects. It is very difficult to maintain a sense of objectivity, fairness, and evenhandedness in political topics.

Social sciences and history try to hold stories in check, separating the genres into facts and opinion, identifying sources, and justifying value judgments. However, as soon as we seek to describe in beautiful language and discuss how we feel or should feel about people and events, there is a shift toward literary expression.

We want to enjoy a well-written history with vivid examples and personalities, not a drab litany of names, dates, and places! History can be done as good as a novelist could do, but if so should we worry?

History, in short, is a minefield of stories, real and imagined, and in-between, fabricated and documented, ready to be exploited, ready to be exploded! That is what makes it so interesting and challenges us to observe the content closely and separate out the wheat from the chaff.

KEY QUESTIONS TO CONSIDER, APPLY, AND EVOLVE

- Is a story different from history? How so?
- Is the structure of history reporting like or unlike storytelling?
- How do we decide what parts of a story are fact or fiction?
- When do we discount the contents of a story and when do we believe it?
- Are there clues to 'making up' or embellishing stories?
- How do people give reports that improve tales well told?
- How do historians combat fibbing and exaggeration?
- When and why do historians and social scientists fall prey to untruthful stories?
- When and why do people 'improve and dramatize' true stories?
- Is the idea of a story fundamental to teaching and learning history, and if so, how can we increase critical thinking in checking sources and storytellers?

NOTES

1. White, H. (1980). "The value of narrativity in the representation of reality" *Critical Inquiry* 7(Autumn), 1, 283.

2. After the twins were abandoned by their parents, legend has it that they were raised by the Wolf going on to found the Roman Republic. This is a fifth-century BC bronze in the Capitoline Museum in Rome. This image is not subject to Freedom of Panorama restrictions. The subject of this image (or other media file) is in the public domain because its copyright has expired/Wikipedia commons.

3. Mieke, B. (1985). *Narratology. Introduction to the Theory of Narrative.* Toronto: Toronto University Press.

4. White, Hayden (2010). *The Fiction of Narrative: Essays on History, Literature, and Theory, 1957–2007.* Baltimore: Johns Hopkins University Press.

5. Daly, Chris (2009). "The historiography of journalism history: Part 2: Toward a new theory" *American Journalism* 26(1), 148–155.

6. Angeletti, Norberto, and Alberto Oliva (2004). Magazines That Make History: Their Origins, Development, and Influence, covers Time, Der Spiegel, Life, Paris Match, National Geographic, Reader's Digest, ¡Hola!, and People.

7. UNESCO: Story-based inquiry; a manual for investigative journalists (PDF). Manual. UNESCO Publishing. Retrieved 27 August 2011.

8. *NYTimes*, 1 November 2019, p. B3.

9. Paine, T. (1776). *Common Sense: An Address to the Inhabitants of America, Pamphlet.*

10. Gelfert, A. (2014). *A Critical Introduction to Testimony.* London: Bloomsbury Academic.

11. Shieber, J. (2015). *Testimony: A Philosophical Introduction.* London: Routledge.

12. Curley, Jeffrey. "iCivics Celebrates Gaming Milestone" *iCivics.* Retrieved 19 July 2011.

13. Lowenthal, D. (2000). Dilemmas and delights of learning history. In Peter N. Stearns; Peters Seixas; Sam Wineburg (Eds.), *Knowing Teaching and Learning History, National and International Perspectives* (pp. 63–81). New York & London: New York University Press.

14. Marwick, A. (2001). *The New Nature of History: Knowledge, Evidence, Language.* London and Houndsmills: Palgrave.

15. According to view A (Carlyle):

Hero-worship is the deepest root of all; the tap-root, from which in a great degree all the rest were nourished and grown.

And now if worship even of a star had some meaning in it, how much more might that of a Hero! Worship of a Hero is transcendent admiration of a Great Man. I say great men are still admirable; I say there is at bottom, nothing else for one higher than himself dwells in the breast of man. It is to this hour, and at all hours, the vivifying influence in man's life. Religion I find stand upon it; not Paganism only, but far higher and truer religions,—all religion hitherto unknown. Hero-worship, heartfelt prostrate admiration, submission, burning, boundless, for a noblest godlike Form of Man,—is not that the germ of Christianity itself? The greatest of all Heroes is One—whom we do not name here! . . .

Or coming into lower, less unspeakable provinces, is not all Loyalty akin to religious Faith also? Faith is loyalty to some inspired teacher, some spiritual Hero. And what therefore is loyalty proper, the life breath of all society, but an effluence of Hero-worship, submissive admiration for the truly great? Society is founded on Hero-worship . . . (Thomas Carlyle [1966,1873)] On Heroes, Hero-Worship and the Heroic in History, Lincoln, Nebraska: University of Nebraska Press, pp. 11–12)

According to view B (Marx):

From my antipathy (hatred) for any cult of the individual, I never made public during the existence of the First International the numerous addresses from various countries which recognized my merits and which annoyed me. . . . Engels and I first joined the secret society of Communists on the condition that everything making for superstitious worship of authority would be deleted from its statute. (Letter to Wilhelm Bloss from Karl Marx cited in Secret Speech Delivered by First Party Secretary at the Twentieth Party Congress of the Communist Party of the Soviet Union, February 25, 1956, https://digitalarchive.wilsoncenter.org/document/115995)

The history of all hitherto existing society is the history of class struggles. Freeman and slave, patrician and plebeian, lord and serf, guild-master and journeyman, in a word, oppressor and oppressed, stood in constant opposition to one another, carried on an uninterrupted, now hidden, now open fight, a fight that each time ended, either in a revolutionary reconstitution of society at large, or in the common ruin of the contending classes. (Karl Marx, The Communist Manifesto [1848] p.1)

16. Benjamin, Jules R. (2019). *A Student's Guide to History* (14th ed.). Boston, MA: Bedford/St. Martins.

17. White, Hayden (1987). *The Content of the Form: Narrative Discourse and Historical Representation*. Baltimore and London: Johns Hopkins University Press. pp. 1 (Barthes), 104–141.

18. White H., Autumn, (1980). "The Value of Narrativity in the Representation of Reality" *Critical Inquiry* 7(1), 283–293.

19. Norrick, Neal R. (2000). *Conversational Narrative: Storytelling in Everyday Talk*. Amsterdam & Philadelphia: John Benjamins Publishing Company.

20. Tosh, John (2010). *The Pursuit of History* (5th ed.). New York and London: Routledge.

21. Carr, E. H. (2001with a new introduction by Richard J. Evans.) *What is History?* Basingstoke: Palgrave Macmillan.

22. Bruner, Jerome S. (1986). *Actual Minds, Possible Worlds*. Cambridge, MA: Harvard University Press.

23. Cronon, William (2013). "Storytelling" *American Historical Review* 118(1), 1–19. online, Discussion of the impact of the end of the Cold War upon scholarly research funding, the impact of the Internet and Wikipedia on history study and teaching, and the importance of storytelling in history writing and teaching.

24. Presnell, Jenny L. (2012). *The Information-Literate Historian: A Guide to Research for History Students*. Oxford, UK: Oxford University Press.

25. White, H. (1973). *Metahistory: The Historical Imagination in 19th Century Europe*. Baltimore: Johns Hopkins University Press.

Chapter 5

Lenses

Multiple Perspectives in the Teaching and Learning of History

> The best ideas emerge when very different perspectives meet.
>
> —Frans Johansen

OVERVIEW

Lenses are all about seeing the world in multiple ways, at least a few of which are different from your own. In addition, they are about adopting and adapting perspectives of "others" that aid you in occupying shoes of those with varied personal and world views.

HEADLINE!

Independent rights experts urge US to address systemic racism and racial bias. UN News Global perspective human stories, June 5, 2020

I. INTRODUCTION

Lenses are placed in a frame to look through adjusted to your eyesight, but also come in many others sizes, shapes, and tints, now even adjustable for degrees of lightness and darkness. The way we define lenses in history alludes to both our view and our viewpoint. So, consider the following definition to use in history and social science:

"A device or phenomenon (such as a gravitational field) that causes light or other radiation to converge or diverge by an action analogous to that of a lens."

Here is a wholly scientific definition that does little to help us think about a lens giving better, clearer, and more objective eyesight, and a sense of perception when viewing events through a variety of lenses, tinted, clear, or clouded, as in real-life history. We all usually prefer the proverbial "rose-tinted lenses." So, let's think about lenses as providing for different viewpoints, clashing testimony, and multiple perspectives. Think about lenses that offer better focus, clearer views, and wider illumination in the dark wells of historical evolution.

Let's consider lenses a science of viewing through a diverse array of people's perspectives and with varying degrees of insight.

II. WHAT ARE LENSES AND PERSPECTIVES?

Human beings always have different perspectives toward other people, places, and events, particularly when there are biases, conflicts of interpretation and judgments. Perspectives, which we will refer to as "lenses" in this chapter give us room for metaphor and meaning growing out of historical and social events, as in "looking at the world through rose-colored lenses."

This is an optical way of saying that some see the world as a bright and happy place, while others have a much darker vision. We can also play with light and darkness, with history sometimes emerging from the dark into the light, other times, descending from light into darkness.

People naturally prefer a lighter, brighter, rosy picture, but there are a number of doom and naysayers around. But people also like dichotomies between light and dark, as in good or evil, sometimes ascribing two sides to a clash that is far more complicated in real history, and life!

The lens you are looking through is shaped by many forces and situations, your personality, location, setting, culture, political philosophy, and national or international loyalties. The eyeglass may also promote nearsightedness or farsightedness, clear or cloudy vision, and on special occasions telephoto and wide-angle capabilities.

The ways in which you see the world and specific events may raise or harm your level of understanding what is happening and why it is happening. Lack of understanding may turn out to be very costly to you personally and to the national unit you owe or believe you owe, allegiance. Some have suggested a global clash of civilizations as a key to understanding history.[1]

Lenses may be applied to events, but the arts may also attempt to shape the way lenses are used to imagine or represent events. The Internet and theater, the arts and music, may offer potent and memorable lenses to view people and events, perhaps on occasion more powerful than historical writing or social science analysis. In effect, the artist is providing a lens for reviewing the past and present in dramatic and emotional ways frowned upon by social scientists.

In most cases, the lens you adopt is from your own experience and lifestyle. You are a witness in a place and time, a position, and you as part of society, your upbringing and affiliations. But there is also a lens that is you role-playing by placing yourself, as best you can, in another's place, outside your own context. This takes discipline and perspective about building and changing lenses purposely to step into someone else's shoes,[2] NOT your own.[3]

Thinking consciously about "seeing" others really changes your perspective, indeed! In any case, the lens or perspective through which you, as a witness, view the world around you, shapes what you notice, and how you interpret events. Unless of course you opt to be another, a "them" and not an "us."[4]

III. A LESSON IN PERSPECTIVES

So, let's examine two Japanese depictions of Commodore Matthew Perry (1794–1858) of the U.S. Navy, the fellow who played a key role in opening Japan to trade and traffic in the mid-nineteenth century. In 1853, Commodore Perry, in command of four ships, entered Tokyo harbor and demonstrated his technologically advanced firepower by blowing away some dock buildings. This caused a sensation among Japanese leaders who felt they were left behind in terms of world contacts and military power.

In 1854, the commodore returned to negotiate a trade treating with Japan precipitating the decline of the Shogun government that had kept the country closed off for the most part from the rest of the world. Japanese contact with the West and America is a wonderful case study of seeing others through different lenses.[5]

Below you are asked to compare two depictions of the commodore by Japanese artists with an American photograph. This is an exercise in viewpoints and lenses as the three images are quite different. The Japanese artists show Perry through their lenses: status, military symbols, and designs are presented in Asian art styles. In the first image, figure 5.1, by a Japanese artist, Kawabaran, the Western admiral is wearing a Japanese-style hat and holding a ceremonial sword, with correct treatment of his uniform epaulets. His eyebrows and mustache hair are emphasized, and his ears are quite large. All writing is in Japanese characters. The overall effect is very much to present

Figure 5.1 Commodore Matthew Perry by Japanese Artist, Kawaraban, 1845. Rysenoji Treasure Museum, Kyoto, Japan, Print 30-044. COMMORDORE MATTHEW PERRY by a Japanese artist, KAWARABAN Osaka, Japan (1854) Print 30-044, Sensoji Temple Treasure Museum, Tokyo, courtesy of Wikipedia Commons.

Figure 5.2 Commodore Matthew Perry, USN, Photograph by Matthew Brady, 1856–1858. MetMuseum of Art, released to the public domain/Wikipedia, for life plus 100 years. Photograph of: COMMORDORE MATTHEW PERRY, USN BY MATHEW BRADY (circa 1856–1858) Source: METMUSEUM.ORG.

Perry in Asian fashion but remaining true to his general features, perhaps with too large a nose and chin.

Figure 5.2, a Western photo of the commodore, presents him clean-shaven, nice head of hair, and wearing his official uniform with epaulets and a clear expression of status as a high-ranking military personality. He offers a rather somber demeanor, baggy eyes, and a lack of emotion, posing stiffly in the nineteenth-century manner. Yet a third image, figure 5.3, again by a Japanese artist, working in quite a different but still Asian style, shows the admiral very much like the photographic expression in terms of emotion, but set within a cleaner, more Western style, or perhaps somewhere between Japanese designs and Western. The uniform is brightly colored in Japanese colors and designs obscuring his military status.

These images demonstrate how lenses can operate as openings to understanding how other cultures see us and depict us. The lenses could be reversed with U.S. artists depictions of others, then broadened to cross-cultural exchanges of art, photography, that show efforts at accurate presentations that somehow fall short of the original and lean toward styles and ideas that characterize and shape one culture's view over another. Perhaps it takes time for a true meeting of art styles that promote cultural understanding.

Research a set of images of your own character from history. Choose that raise questions of cultural contact among and between peoples through mutual attempts at accurate representation

a. Witness

All of us are witnesses to history, sometimes even eyewitnesses. Where we are at an historical moment can influence our view of an event for a very long time, resting in our memory banks, often with strong feelings attached. 9/11, when two passenger jets were forcefully crashed into the World Trade Center in New York, on September 11, 2001, was a New York event that became a worldwide event through the auspices of local and global communication networks.

Levels of emotion can be very high in New York when 9/11 is brought up but many places and nations participated in the tragic event by TV transmission, radio, Internet, and other channels. The hijackers of the aircraft also undoubted experienced deep emotions, although this was hardly discussed. The "enemy" view is often overlooked or simply assumed to be hateful. Beware of one-sided witnesses when you try to answer why the attackers struck the World Trade Towers.

Thus, modern communications can help people across a wide swath of the world become witnesses to events at great distance. Eyewitnesses have

Figure 5.3 Commodore Matthew Perry of the U.S. Navy by Unknown Japanese Artist, 1854. Public domain, according to copyright laws of Japan. COMMODORE MATHEW PERRY OF THE U.S. NAVY (1854) artist unknown. Commodore Perry by unknown Japanese artist.

an advantage or disadvantage in being there close at hand. This may be an historical problem because the eyewitness sighting may be too traumatic and destructive to render a balanced interpretation of what is happening. On the other hand, close-up vision may offer detailed knowledge not sensed at all by witnesses geographically distant.[6]

Yet, the roles of both eyewitness and witness yield understandings and emotions that would be absent if you were not connected to events. Someone wandering the jungle on 9/11 would only hear about events third hand and would be much less likely to experience an emotional effect of much strength. They would be unlikely to see the towers fall on TV or video.[7]

A broad range of eyewitness accounts and witness reactions would probably provide a much fuller picture of perspectives than more limited account through narrow lenses. For example, we tend to know quite a bit about European conquest and the slave trade, but almost all from one side. We might ask for African witnesses, royals or commoners, and we may find interesting materials, like the letters from African kings and queens to European monarchs encroaching their territories. In a letter dating to 1526, from King Afonso (tribal name was Mvemba a Nzinga) he was the son of Manikongo (Mwene Kongo), the fifth king of the Kongo dynasty. The king of the Kongo was a powerful monarch with a huge territory but had problems once Europeans arrived, mostly from Portugal. He had written to the king of Portugal complaining of the behavior of traders, that is,

> Each day the traders are kidnapping our people—children of this country, sons of our nobles and vassals, even people of our own family. This corruption and depravity are so widespread that our land is entirely depopulated. We need in this kingdom only priests and schoolteachers, and no merchandise, unless it is wine and flour for Mass. It is our wish that this Kingdom not be a place for the trade or transport of slaves.
>
> Many of our subjects eagerly lust after Portuguese merchandise that your subjects have brought into our domains. To satisfy this inordinate appetite, they seize many of our black free subjects. . . . They sell them. After having taken these prisoners [to the coast] secretly or at night . . . As soon as the captives are in the hands of white men they are branded with a red-hot iron.[8]

The African king's complaints of kidnapping and corruption fit in with the general picture of European invasion and slave trading. He complains that they need schoolteachers and priests, not slave traders, and explains that his subjects want trade goods and are willing to sell prisoners to obtain them from the Portuguese. Afonso's lenses are mostly negative, but interesting indicating a shift to the outside world for goods, and a willingness to Europeanize, for which rewards do not seem forthcoming. His letter was written in Portuguese and is quite literate and communicative, further evidence of assimilating European languages and faiths.

The Portuguese king and merchants seem to have a very different set of lenses focusing on making money to buy captives and selling trade goods to the Kongo people.

Like a trial, witnesses are of key importance in history. Their perspectives really matter, as do their locations and roles. Witnesses can be friendly or hostile, or in-between, and this matters considerably as it colors their descriptions of events, as well as their interpretations. The witness should always be questioned closely before making any rash and quick decisions, or judgments.

This is what makes history interesting, complicated, and suspicious!

b. Position and Role

The position of an eyewitness or witness, how close or far from the event, and their personal and public values determine how and what they see. Descriptions can be full or partial depending on actual physical location and pre-diagnostic values. If someone is strongly conservative or liberal, nationalistic (and for which country) or deeply prejudiced, then their accounts may vary considerably from each other.

A Saudi prince, a British socialist, and an American general might very well have different takes, use contrasting lenses, to describe and interpret events on 9/11. Who is heroic and for what reasons takes on specific values at this point and sets value judgments into motion that will likely clash. One's role, like position, can greatly influence how we see events that impact us even at a distance even through electronic news media.

Roles (jobs, status, rank, and gender) also shape our lenses, with ordinary people and extraordinary people, like the tower occupants, and local firemen, diplomats, and leaders expressing a wide variety of perspectives and "colors" in defining their relationship to an event. Who we hold as valuable leaders, and how we interpret heroism lead to judgments that can be disturbing and satisfying at the same time.[9]

For example, many argue that the true heroines and heroes of 9/11 in New York were the ordinary people in the towers and surrounding buildings who risked their lives to save others. Firemen and police might be classified through a lens for "ordinary heroes." Leadership at the time does not seem to have produced very many memorable heroes as potential statues in parks.

Roles really matter in this event giving special perspective to those directly involved that almost no other people played in this event.

The lenses you are wearing can drastically change not only how you view events but how you feel about them. Your viewpoint may begin with negative or positive feelings about an event like 9/11, an attack that almost immediately causes worries and stirs prejudices against the perpetrators. We want to know their origins and politics and why they are engaged in aggressive violence against a building in New York. We do not understand the reasons for the attack and want to know a lot more, but our feelings are so strong that we cannot handle historical analysis. We miss the reasons, because we would like to demonize the evil-doers.

Worse yet, our role, and our placement, matters. If we are New Yorkers, and working as police, firemen, sanitation, and other city services, we are needed on site and get to see upfront in our roles the horror of buildings collapsing and the rain of destruction across much of lower Manhattan.

Our witnessing, our roles, and our placement combine into very strong feelings about the event, personalized and dramatic. Yet, this may not make us the best historians in this instance. Our emotions are true to ourselves but do not necessarily help us to understand the evolution and purpose of this attack led mostly by a nation allied with the United States, Saudi Arabia.

c. Upbringing, Affiliations, Ideologies, and Religions

Witnesses bring with them many lenses, many perspectives, shaped by their growing up in a particular culture and social network. Each of us belongs to many subgroups, subcultures, and play many roles in our lives. Each role and activity provides different and enriching perspectives, even if it is only learning to play the piano, joining a soccer team, identifying with a political party, growing up with a second language.

Each piece of our roles deepens our understanding and perspective on other facets of life, and without these experiences, our views would be much thinner and we would miss details, and maybe overlook meaning. Music education sharpens our hearing and we begin to think about different kinds of music: folk, rock, classical, jazz, bebop, and so on. Our horizon has expanded so when we go to a movie or a concert, we pick up bits and pieces that others miss. We realize that we might have many more and richer lenses than some of our friends.[10]

A multiplicity of roles increases our value as observers who might be capable of seeing through many lenses. We will be more attentive to the words and sounds we hear if we are musically trained, and have insight to the value of sounds in history (rarely discussed, alas).

But as much as written documents, sounds are a part of history, and that includes songs, stories told aloud, music and notation, and recorded speeches. Although in French, nearly everyone in the world would recognize the Marseillaise, written in 1792, a song that became the French national anthem, and witnessing or teaching the film *Casablanca*, realize that the song has emotional depth especially when sung by patriots in a bar scene to counter Nazi officers singing "Deutschland Uber Alles," a contest of wills, values, and identification, expressed through music.

Upbringing and socialization count in playing with lenses, and these are underpinned by affiliations, ideologies, and religious faith as well as other beliefs and identifications. Depending on levels of faith and identification with causes, one's loyalties and affiliations may yield a rich set of perceptions on some problems. How you feel about the institution of slavery in the Old South, pre-Civil War, will color almost all your views of the current issues of racism and political gerrymandering the descendant states of the Confederacy.

Which side, North or South, your ancestors were on might determine which lenses you use to interpret current events in the United States, which political party you vote for, how you see African Americans, and whether or not you vote in the next election. Your religion might work against the lenses you would like to employ to see social problems and political choices, but it might also work for them. Historical influences can run very deep in populations shaping views of history dozens or hundreds, or even thousands of years later.

If you are a liberal or conservative, Socialist or Libertarian, the tint on your spectacles studying civil war may cloud over or become crystal clear. Your interpretation of events will depend very much on how you identify your historical loyalties, and result in very different present and future decisions. Your choice of colors viewing the past will change the history to come! Loyalties that endure are key choices in historical development and social organization, determining how we see our roles and how we see "others."

d. Standing in Others' Shoes

Thus, who you are, where you come from, how you were brought up and where add up to a package of identifications and views: favorite teams, feelings about religion (if relevant) educational activities, social status and standing, who belong with "us" and who with "others" political ideology (if any) or party identity (if any or none). That is the historical you as a witness, and role, and reporter. It is not easy stepping away, or out of your most comfortable views and identity to take a fresh look at history by standing in others' shoes.[11]

But to be a fine history/social science teacher and historian, you must go beyond your self and your comfort zone in viewing people, places, and events. You may already be an excellent witness or eyewitness on occasion, but until you adopt a strategy of looking at the world as another person from another culture and perspective, you will always see events from one side mainly. And historically speaking, that is a major problem of perspective and optics.

At a minimum, we need to adopt at least one contrasting or supplemental view, and if bold indeed, hopefully a disturbing role that yields insider knowledge and feeling about an event. Literally stand in the place of another and look at events from their perspective, through their lens. Better yet, look at several others; views, a range of others, not just ours. Experiment and experience what events and issues look like from the people we have overlooked or walked away from so as to avoid disturbance. It is always most comfortable to keep our view, our community view, our national view over anyone else to make sure our side always looks good.

Others' views might disturb you, but will add immeasurably to your understanding of events. Nothing may look the same to you and you will find out that others have humanity and viewpoints of their own, and even more upsetting, feelings that may diametrically oppose your own. Sitting in another's place is no easy but it is actually how we can learn history with all the warts on from at least two or more "sides."

Examples abound for every subject, world, United States, economics, civics, anthropology as there are contrasting views in each and every one of these, usually overlooked in favor of endorsing the least disturbing account from the most satisfying and comforting sources.

For example, seek out the Filipino account of the liberation of the Philippines by the United States; seek out the Persian view of the Ancient Athenians; seek out the Aztec view of the Spanish invasion of their empire; seek out African views of colonial settlements in the eighteenth and nineteenth centuries; seek out the Aboriginal view of Australian conquest and settlement; seek out the Algerian reaction to French colonization; seek out Hong Kong's citizens views of interference by the People's Republic of China. There are always other views with which you can agree or disagree, and we can always argue about the hue of the view, dark and cloudy, bright and rosy, or clear and sunny.[12]

Develop a rounded view of history, two-sided or more, that gives a bigger picture from several sources and perspectives.[13] Cross-check accounts, add them together, divided and multiply, and work to create your own history lens on issues and cultures usually viewed from only one perspective, ours.

IV. WHY DO VIEWS AND VIEWPOINTS OFTEN DIFFER?

a. Historical Context

Before diving into a topic, think about when and where the author lived, and the times in which she or he was a participant. Each time produces its own anxieties and satisfactions, its own rewards and punishments, and its own "atmosphere" if you will.

The overall "atmosphere" can deeply influence a reporter, witness, or eyewitness. A document contemporary with a time period incorporates all kinds of influences some of which the present-day reader may notice, but others may be too subtle or different for immediate notice. Language itself changes, and meanings drift away from time to time, so language itself and translations of language provide a sense of the character/author, the class and educational level, and the temper of the times.[14]

A context may be peaceful or warlike, experiencing economic growth and prosperity or dire poverty and this can make a great deal of difference in the way someone, an eyewitness, reports on her experience. For example, the delightful tales of the *Decameron* by Giovanni Boccaccio written in the fourteenth century in Florence, Italy, begins with a dire account of a horrifying plague ravaging town and countryside.

This can be regarded as a factual, real document, but then the author uses the crisis and segues into a series of one hundred morality tales told by rather well-educated young people to one another after they flee into the countryside to escape the plague experience.

The entire series of tales provides deep insights into the Renaissance way of thinking about many topics ranging from religion and morality to social status and political standing. Though literature, this book can be used as historical evidence even when it crosses genre lines from autobiography to storytelling.

The plague sets a context of tremendous crisis and disorientation for society because people almost died on the spot leaving friends and family to fend for themselves in a society that generally cared for one another under normal circumstances. Like a war, or economic collapse, disasters can set the tone for historical reporting, artistic production, literature, and the overall mood of an entire population.

When teaching a document, we need to ask what sort of times surrounded it and how events influenced the artist, author, composer, or producer of the account. Documents do not simply arrive from nowhere, although much social studies and history teaching presents documentation without much context at all, without much thinking about the reporter's status and education, and without much attention to language and mood.

b. Personal History

Just as context impacts on historical production and expression, so does the eyewitness' personal characteristics and evolution matter greatly in how a story or event is described and judged.

Students and teachers may read a speech by Abraham Lincoln without knowing much of anything about him, but he was a rather remarkable individual and brought with him many unusual talents to the White House. He also grew up relatively poor in Illinois achieving a good classical education with considerable difficulty yet developed into a first-rate author and speechmaker. He wrote his own speeches by the way.

Lincoln made to the presidency by a circuitous route, an unlikely winner at a certain stage when he boldly opposed war with Mexico. This cost him his election at the time and he had to rebuild his candidacy slowly and carefully. He became an active political leader during a tense and conflicted context in which abolitionist opposing slavery were increasingly angry at the practice of slavery in the South. Lines of political belief were hardening and there were threats of conflict, secession, and savage attacks on leaders from both sides with those in the middle losing ground.

Lincoln managed to weather the political infighting and succeeded a pro-slavery president, Buchanan, who had fanned the flames of conflict while in office. Thus the context of Lincoln's life was framed by issues of slavery and conflict between North and South, which were drifting into two different countries, and divided loyalties. The United States still reflects these divisions to this day although the overall context is different or has morphed into different forms.

Personal history, one that is part of historical context, both reflects and helps develop the flow of events. While few of us can change the course of history, all of us are part of it, and some of us can be of considerable influence at the right time and place, in the right role for the time. We can prepare a personal history following tried and true historical methods.[15]

The point is that as teachers and learners we should be aware, and SUSPICIOUS, of hard and fast conclusions until we learn a bit about the witnesses to history, and make sense of their language, and ideas, at least partially identifying their probable status and views. Noticing details, especially feelings, in seeing through different lenses is vitally important in understanding events.

c. Passions and Pressures

Passionate belief is a wonderful thing under some circumstances and we need to locate the origins and note the expressions that arise from deep feelings. Passion may be positive and loving, but also hateful and hurtful, and we must be careful in judging the value and veracity of a witness and recounter of events.

Passion may arise from deep-seated beliefs positive and negative that will help us understand the temper of the times, and the motivations of historical actresses and actors. The stronger the passions and the more powerful the pressures, the more we should worry about the reports and accounts coming out of a time and place.[16]

Thus, reading the passionate work of a slaveholder defending that institution, or a Quaker attacking slavery, the more we should seek to balance accounts from several sources, and from competing ideologies. For a balanced overview, we at least need passionate accounts from slaves and ex-slaves, slaveholders, anti-slavery abolitionists, a few middle roaders, and perhaps a couple of foreign visitors just to see how outsiders saw the U.S. path to the Civil War. This is a lot of work but well worth the pressure because it provides a range of perspectives, each with a different lens that adds up to a fairly comprehensive whole of the context.

Middle observers and outsiders may yield more objective input than those directly involved in the conflict and more so than those with deeply passionate pro or con views of the institution of slavery. We must also delve into issues of racism and gender in reporting about the civil war, attitudes that go into the roots of American experience and are still relevant today in different forms, within a different context.

Personality and passion still matter now, and will always matter when dealing with perspectives. Many authors and reporters hide their feelings and keep their lenses within dark and shaded eyeglass cases because they would prefer to sound objective and hide their inner values from observers. This is what makes the tasks of understanding history so interesting and so fraught with conflict and hidden or understated meaning. Views differ due to context, upbringing, experiences, and ideological beliefs that shape how and why historical documents are produced.

d. Conflicts and Actions

Historical observers and writers may also be part of the action. They are participant observers, and the context of the times will dictate not only their reports, but their political views and behavior. Some of the eyewitnesses and witnesses stand away from the debates and clashes, viewing events from an armchair or behind a camera.

These history reporters may see themselves as separated from and complaining about issues ignored by supposedly objective people and events involving gender, subcultures, and issues such as the environment. Where are lenses focused on women's roles?[17] Where are lenses focused on multicultural groups?[18] Where are lenses aimed at the environmental problems that currently beset us and will continue into the future?[19]

However, as teachers and learners, we need to ask a lot of questions about the lenses through which observers view events, and how these can impact the final accounts when put together. Being a participant has an advantage over the armchair witnesses since they were really present at key conversations, decisions, and actions. However, direct experience may increase the flow of adrenalin and excitement within great events, obscuring other's views, and dramatizing what has happened in more emotional ways than may be justified.

Participation increases a sense of self-importance and a sense of emotional power.

By contrast the languid armchair observer, reading or rereading accounts, may be too distant, too analytical, and too detached to provide anything but an action by action bloodless list of events. This detached and analytical accounting is precisely what many professional historians and textbook writers seek to achieve, leaving emotion and judgment to the readers, students, and teachers.

We need both participant observers with passions who react to the pressures of the time, and outsider or analytic historians who calmly add up and compare events as they prepare their version of the story. The story itself is open to question, change, and revision, at every level, depending on the trustworthiness of eyewitnesses, the availability of sound and film recordings, and the cross-checking of sources, and the interpretations by a range of professional social scientists and historians.

Particularly in conflict situations and contexts, we need multiple kinds of actors and actions, some from participants who are part of the event, and some from outsiders and the impartial who are observing the flow of events as they see them.

No one source, lens, eyewitness, witness, or historian should be trusted completely in developing a narrative, a time line, a documentary, or even a literary reinterpretation of significant people, places, and events.

Multiple lenses should always be adopted for viewing and reviewing history and a sense of suspicion or at least reasonable doubt should direct you to a series of tentative interpretations of history, with even more care practice in rendering value judgments on which decisions were right or wrong or neither or in-between as a time period chronologically ends.

V. WHEN IS AGREEMENT ON LENSES AND PERSPECTIVE MORE LIKELY OR LESS LIKELY?

Lenses tend to color interpretations, bright and clear, rosy and happy, dark and sinister. Often in history, lenses may also offer different views, and sometimes clashing views of the same people and events. Lenses tend to converge when there is relative peace and prosperity, but diverge and conflict when cultures see others in a hostile and disapproving way. For example, does the population take global warming seriously when scientific evidence is provided or do they avoid the subject, or reject the claims totally?[20]

We must practice caution and suspicion before we leap into a political or cultural dispute, keeping an open mind to making sense of the evidence.

a. Multiple Eyewitnesses

If we have more than one set of eyewitnesses, and more than one view of an event, then we have a better chance at a balanced and truthful understanding of an event.

Concordance, seeking agreement on facts and reasons, is a major contribution by historians to the story of the past. The fewer witnesses we have, and the more one-sided, the more we should worry about balance and bias.

Unfortunately, in many cases, we only have one-sided and/or culturally and/or politically biased accounts that may bring more confusion and conflict in drawing conclusions. Great care should be taken. If conflict is involved than we must be wary of either side's description of events, much less the conclusions that are drawn up.

Conclusions should be tentative and reflect the evidence fairly, admitting error, bias, and missing pieces. A good teaching historian or social scientist should outline and identify her/his biases and theoretical orientation at the start of a narrative or investigation. For example, Custer's last stand comes from potentially partial witnesses and eyewitnesses. Accounts include Mrs. Custer's biography of her husband but she was not part of the battle.

The general could not help us since he died in the battle. The Native American story was dictated to writers and painted on skins so we have some inkling of their story. But even here, there are problems with pride, victory, and cultural bias. Thus, each lens presents issues to solve, and we must carefully tiptoe through the messy evidence. The whole episode in history is an example of clashing cultures. So, let's be especially careful of battle statistics about how many were wiped out at Little Bighorn.

Putting together outside sources, native American accounts, surviving scouts and soldier's accounts, archeological investigations of the battlefield, and historical theories, we may develop a reasonable lens on what happened, who and how many were killed, and why it happened at all.

b. Shared Values and Common Loyalties

Where values are shared by eyewitnesses and historians, there is generally relatively strong agreement on describing events, interpreting action, and drawing tentative conclusions. Conveying the results can be summarized and built into a solid narrative or story.

Within a society or nation, values are usually shared by all or most of the citizens, building shared lenses of life and culture. Much of the sharing of stories, traditions, and holidays is done through school textbooks and teaching, government programs of remembrance and honoring outstanding citizens. For example, the U.S. government has built memorials to Civil War monuments, World War II armed service personnel, and Vietnam War veterans. Christopher Columbus is honored by national and local holidays, although many monuments now challenged by proponents of Indigenous People's Day.[21]

Who is chosen to be honored can range from ordinary people who gave their lives for their nation to heroic champions of causes. Often, individual statues demonstrate and inspire loyalty to cause and country. These may be put up in parks, near offices, on government land and buildings, or sometimes privately sponsored, or cosponsored with government assistance.

However, the problem with values and history is that societies change with the times, and new values, sometimes conflicting, sometimes novel, shift how people once viewed people, places, and events. Thus, parks across almost any nation contain statues and art from the past that no longer reflect shared values and may become bones or lumps of contention within and among citizens.

Outside societies and nations barely have a toehold on the interior life of most nations, although ethnic change and historical contributions recognize the value of outsiders, particularly when their values and ours match.[22]

For instance, statues are one of my favorite subjects because they symbolize who is honored and who is left out. In Chicago, which has a large Polish population, there are days devoted to Pulaski and Kosciusko, both migrant generals from Poland who fought on the side of the American revolution. A bridge in New York honors Kosciusko though most students have trouble with the spelling.

One particular contentious era in U.S. history dates back to the period after the Civil War. During the "Jim Crow" era after Reconstruction, much of the South regained political power and began putting up statues to Civil War Confederate generals and leaders. The confederate flag was often flown at State Capitals, Richmond, Birmingham, and Jackson, but these did not appeal to common loyalties or the descendants of the slaves freed and given the vote after the Civil War or to Northern citizens.

After the Civil Rights movements of the 1960s and the passage of voting rights act, more and more objections were raised to statues enshrining leaders who defended a breakaway group of states who voted to secede from the majority and form their own country. These competing values and loyalties are still being fought on many fronts, with a great deal of argument about issues of race in an era of changing values and views of confederate statues.

Changing values in the last thirty to fifty years have also reshaped views of the role and status of women.

There are many fewer statues to female heroines and leaders than there are to men. Thus, there is a movement to rectify the situation and create many more statues and monuments to honor women, but there are issues of both race and gender that appear when the authorities seek to honor historical figures.

A recent case illuminates continuing arguments about whom to honor and how, demonstrating that loyalties are divided across U.S. society. This is a proposal to build a statue (now erected) in Central Park, New York, to honor women suffragettes, but also to include at least one African American figure to balance out the white representatives.

The monument was narrowly approved by the City Design Commission by a vote of 6–3 for unveiling in August 2020 to commemorate the 100th anniversary of the Nineteenth Amendment to the U.S. Constitution giving women the right to vote. Issues of race and accuracy were raised that led to the inclusion of Sojourner Truth who was African American but never met Susan or Elizabeth either, since both supported only white women for the vote.

The three women intended to appear in the statue now include the leaders Elizabeth Cady Stanton, Susan B. Anthony, and Sojourner Truth, who was a freed slave. The suffragette statue was proposed after criticism that there were so few statues in Central Park of real historical women who worked at winning the right to vote. Sojourner Truth was proposed after criticism that women of other races needed to be included for their valuable contributions in lobbying for the vote.

Thus, what were once shared values form male heroes and/or perhaps repressed values in favor of honoring women and African Americans has morphed in recent times into a more inclusive and egalitarian value in favor of interracial and multiethnic statuary representations reflecting race and gender that reflect current views.

VI. TAKING NEW PERSPECTIVES

Adopting and adapting new perspectives to the views you are comfortable with can be annoying and even painful. We all live cocooned in a culture that we are familiar with, and deeply value. All of us want to think that our nation, culture, society, and personalities are the best, the greatest, the way things should be for everyone else.

Alas, even with globalization, so called, and international contact increasingly facilitated by world media, most people, including teachers, are surprisingly unaware of and not especially interested in the history and lenses of others. There are many reasons for this basically inward-looking orientation.

Figure 5.4 Proposed Statue of Suggragettes Susan B. Anthony, Elizabeth Cady Stanton, and Sojourner Truth. NYC Design Commission Mockup (2019) by Artist Meredith Bergmann. Proposed Statue of Elizabeth Cady Stanton, Sojourner Truth, and Susan B. Anthony for Central Park, New York City. NYC Design Commission (2019), mock up by artist Meredith Bergmann.

Our concerns tend to focus our lenses on ourselves, family, and livelihood often to the exclusion of big issues in history or even small issues at home. Climate change so called as well as issues of race, gender, ethnicity, immigration, and environment arise daily, weekly, and monthly. Nevertheless, the Climate Big History to come makes us buy newer and more stylish rose-tinted lenses.[23]

a. Examining Attitudes and Worldviews

First, we are part of a series of routines, habits, and communication that is arranged for and plays to our own nation and culture. Even so-called multicultural and diverse societies, empires, and groups tend to look back to historical underpinnings and beliefs that can be traced to the foundations of a people. Language, tradition, law, custom, and history play significant roles in swaddling a people in its own comfortable system of ideas and behaviors.

Second, for historians and social scientists, one of the problems for cultural insider-ness is that it creates ethnocentric attitudes, and encourages seeing everything "not ours" as outside the culture and nation. Alas, ethnocentrism sets up a feeling of superiority to other peoples, and an exotification of those with quite different ways of thinking and doing things. It creates a "them" and "us" division of the world we live in daily.

Third, this attitude of superiority and difference is not a new phenomenon, but it is alas, quite powerful and can breed negative views of others, other cultures, and other systems of government and economics. The assumption of unique cultures is at its root quite wrong and misleading because all cultures have borrowed freely from past and present cultures, and continue to do so at an accelerated rate.

We are all one species, with thousands of years of historical borrowing, and ideas, techniques, and customs have been widely and deeply disseminated, even in the distant past of ancient Israel and Egypt. Religions have crisscrossed the earth and fertilized each other for a thousand years or more.

People have migrated, integrated, and mixed for thousands of years, and all populations have genetic inheritance that is a mix of cultures and peoples. There is no purity of race because there is no race, just a spectrum of skin colors. Once everyone wears a dress or business suit, it becomes quite difficult to discern nationality. Maybe names help?

VII. OPEN-MINDEDNESS TO NEWS AND VIEWS

The point is that within cultures there are a limited range of lenses for looking either inward or outward. If we want to be excellent teachers, there is a strong need to supplement our own culture's view of events with others' views. This might disturb our sense of unique patriotism and superiority, but if we don't do this we really will not understand the flow of events and we will not be able to ask excellent question about all sides to a story.

Therefore, we should seek out and share others' views of history and present-day events. We do not have to believe or endorse anything we read, hear, look at, or interpret, and can and should be wary of quick conclusions especially about which leader or nation or spokesperson is right or wrong on a given issue.

We must study the views presented, as always, and pay close attention to the lens (positive, negative, or neutral?) that is used in grasping events.

We must extend our own comfort zone to include other people's description and accounts to our own representatives, allowing a "benefit of the doubt" to positions taken that may not agree with our own or our government's. In history and social studies, openness can be easily accomplished nowadays by watching two or three news stations coverage of the same events, for instance, BBC, CNN, and Fox News, maybe supplemented with Al Jazeera. Perhaps we can supplement by collecting foreign newspapers in English and/or different languages and translating accounts to compare the positions taken.

Most pointedly, in conflict or controversial situations, we need multiple accounts from many sides, including extending reading and inquiry to reporters seen as enemies. If the United States had paid more attention to North Vietnamese news and Viet Cong reporting during the Vietnam War, many lives might have been saved and our troops would have had more respect for the enemies described as "gooks." The "gooks" turned out to be deeply motivated enemies willing to take great losses to defeat U.S. troops.

a. Suspending Loyalties

A highly creative way of reviewing the lenses of history and social science is to adopt an anthropological neutrality. This method develops by suspending personal loyalties and prejudices to the extent possible, and entering another culture to learn how it sees itself. This takes real work and is not at all easy to pull off because we are all culture bound and conditioned to a considerable extent, but we can exercise our free will to attempt to stand in others' shoes.

Suspending loyalties requires extending a sense of empathy if not sympathy to another culture's or nation's values; their symbols, goals, and system of social relations. This may entail inquiry into other religious systems, different attitudes toward gender and race, and perhaps sharply varying historical trajectories. One nation's history may be quite at odds with our own, and may include a history of conflict and rebellion.

The narratives we have learned must be matched by other narratives, for example, studying Native American stories that contradict and complain about their treatment. This is not necessarily a matter of right, and wrong, but a matter of even deeper meaning, that the story or stories we accept work against each other on the level of explanation and interpretation.

Little Big Man, a most interesting movie about adopting other perspectives tells the story of a boy raised by American settlers, parents killed by an Indian nation's warriors, who is rescued by a different Indian nation and raised in their culture. At one point, Little Big Man, his native name, is rescued yet again by "white folk" who attempt to civilize him in American culture all over again.

Needless to say, Little Big Man hardly knows who and what he is because he is part of two cultures both of which he loves and respects. As the story progresses, Little Big Man's people come into conflict with the U.S. cavalry under General George Custer, and he has to make difficult choices about whom he wants to warn first, and how he will handle the coming conflict.

Many people live in two or more cultures at once, and can manage to combine and adjudicate inconsistencies and disagreements while adapting to the newer society yet maintaining at least a portion of their origins. Immigrant peoples of the world all have to learn how to juggle two or more loyalties and perhaps languages as they try to overcome their own biases and the dominant culture's ethnocentrism.

b. Playing Time and Space Traveler

The ultimate fantasy of contact is perhaps that of time and space traveler. Meeting and greeting fantasies in some science fiction classics contrasts with smash 'em and bash 'em in others. It a kind of contrast between historical contacts where trade and sharing ideas between cultures occurs in one place, yet in another the natives and the newcomers are immediately attacking one another.

Strange creatures are feared aliens who menace human beings in some stories, usually leading to armed conflict, while in others humans and creatures learn from each other and improve relations to the benefit of both. Star Trek tends toward a more open view of others, following philosophical rules for contact and noninterference with more primitive peoples. Most progressive indeed, and a metaphor for contact between peoples!

If only some of the early European explorers had been so open-minded and progressive, history of the Americas and many other places would have been very different. H. G. Wells' *Time Machine* is also a fantasy of culture, but set across time. As the traveler crosses centuries, he sees evidence of great wars and destruction and lands in a far distant future where the human species has been divided into two parts, a passive human-looking people living above ground and a hungry flesh-eating set of mutants living below ground, who are farming the surface dwellers.

In this fantasy, time produces changes we have to adapt to in order to survive, and raises interesting questions about our grasp of historical development. We could argue that crossing time is much like crossing cultures except perhaps the differences are not as noticeable. But crossing backward into early American culture would be quite difficult to adjust to because language and customs would change as would lifestyle and technology. The further back we go even just in say, Virginia, what we take for granted now would start disappearing and we would find ourselves in a culture we would have to learn anew, including its manner of speech and vocabulary. To try this out, ask a school class to read a speech by G. W. Washington, or John Adams aloud and see how much of it they understand without a dictionary.

Thus, playing time and space traveler broadens our viewpoint, adds lenses to our ways of looking, and absorbs many different perspectives that we did not before possess. Cultures, we now realize, shift across time, as well as space, territory as well as boundaries. We are all immigrants in some sense, descended from primitive peoples with simple technologies, and may be part of much more "advanced" culture, if lucky, than our ancestors.

Yet we are still the same species with similar social allegiances, to family, friends, and tribe, and with similar emotions that include anger, love, play, and understanding. As travelers we need to extend and open ourselves to a range of behaviors and beliefs that contrast and/or compare to our own, trying to broaden our views of others while considering ourselves as others to them.

c. Applying Lenses to History from the Many Media We Have and Those to Come

History is most often treated as a reading subject focused on written records: sources and documents. However, documentation also includes art, music, film, and artifacts and other forms of communication from the past. Often these sounds and things and images give us great insight into other peoples' lenses when compared to our own. Going to a museum, concert, or a movie may also be an exercise in using historical lenses. We can literally look into the past, and see how they portrayed themselves and historical events.

If you find it easy to watch a fifty-year-old film that demonstrates continuity of ideas and emotions. We can easily apply our current knowledge to the past and work out the meaning and message the director and producer are sending us from back in time. That implies that our culture has not changed all that much. Relations between people tends to change very slowly, technology tends to change much faster.

Computers have changed a great deal, but toasters are pretty much the same as they were at the point of invention. Even far back into the past, we may be able to identify artifacts by examining probable function and making analogies to implements still in use, like an ax, hammer, or chisel. Stone tools from thousands of years ago, however, are much harder to analogize, but still likely to be understandable.

Art styles are also relatively understandable, although the further back into the past we delve, the more difficult interpretation becomes, mostly because the symbol systems and designs are rather unlike our own. Some cultures produce art and artifacts that are so different from our own because of unique cultural styles that it takes a lot of work for teachers and students to interpret them though that activity may be quite worthwhile in grasping the meaning communicated to use across time and space and cultures.

Trying to interpret and make sense of a striking ancient monument or sculpture, or the work of aboriginal peoples who evolved their own styles can be an engaging mystery worth effort because it expands our lenses to diverse others. Styles can range across abstract, classical, fantastical, literal, and revolutionary. Have lenses on other styles gives us immediate recognition of time and place, at least roughly, and leads to generalizations about cultural dissemination.

For example, Ancient Egyptian art last thousands of years and evolved into a system of beliefs expressed in artistic styles and symbols that are almost instantly recognizable even by beginners. These sculptures represent

Figure 5.5 Statue of Pharaoh Menkaura and Queen Khamerenebty II, Giza Valley Temple of Menkaura, Circa 2548–2530 BC. Donated to Wikipedia shareAlike 2.5 Foundation Keith Schengli-Roberts, Photographer. Statue of Pharaoh Menkaura and Queen Khamerenebty II (circa 2548–2530 BC). Taken from the Giza valley temple of Menkaura. Now in the Museum of Fine Arts, Boston, MA. Keith Schengili-Roberts, Photographer, donated to Wikipedia ShareAlike 2.5 Foundation. Public domain.

an idealized king and queen, very handsome and strong, with attractive bodies posed as a royal couple. Both exude power and beauty, leaders worthy of respect and worship, as well as demonstrating a sense of affection and a loving pose. Though a bit stiff by modern standards, and considering their antiquity, the statues are surprisingly attractive, and send a message to ancient and modern observers alike about leadership and how they want to be viewed by subjects and vassals.

Making statues and portraying strong and warm leaders goes very far back in recorded history, and continues today in much the same manner, though perhaps with different symbols. Why? Because Ancient Egypt stories and styles fascinated Greeks, Romans, and European societies who transmitted these artifacts in books and pictures, and by literally stealing entire temples and monuments to transport to museums around the world. And they are still fascinating us today, which in itself is quite fascinating.

So, let us work toward using a wide variety of lenses across a range of media that includes written works that grabs attention and holds it. Let us not be afraid to use both literature and documents, art and artifacts, music and instruments, fictional and documentary films (as available) to teach students how to view historical evidence broadly and with an open mind to different interpretations.

Above all, lenses, plural especially, invite comparison and contrast of sources, insider and outsider information and interpretation. This leads to a more comprehensive and deeper understanding for students and the historians, who do the hard work of digging for data, using that data to develop a "big picture" of people, places, and events.

To the extent that we are familiar with scientific and historical methods of analysis, we will have a much more satisfying and illuminating contact with both the original sources and the scholarly interpretations. And we will ourselves invent our own judgments of meaning, method, and conclusions, both mechanical and moral. When you recognize your own lenses, and you can adopt the lenses of others, standing in their shoes, you will be well on your way to becoming a critical consumer and teacher.

KEY QUESTIONS TO CONSIDER, APPLY, AND EVOLVE

- Do people always see through "lenses" that may distort history?
- Can we make ourselves conscious of lenses: how and why?
- Are there any lenses we can adopt or adapt that give us other perspectives?
- How do we use outsider lenses and correct for insider lenses?

- Is it easy or difficult to achieve a balanced perspective of either ourselves or others? Why?
- Can ethnocentrism be defeated at least partially, and how might we accomplish that feat?
- Do others see us as we see ourselves?
- How does perspective influence history and historians: do they have issues of perspective too?
- If we are frank about using rosy, dark, or clear glasses in viewing history, are we honest?
- What are multiple lenses and will that solve the problems of storytelling?
- Might we add telescopic or microscopic lenses to our investigations?

NOTES

1. Barber, Benjamin R. (1996). *Jihad vs. McWorld*. Hardcover: Crown; Paperback: Ballantine Books.

2. Huntington, Samuel P. (1996). *The Clash of Civilizations and the Remaking of World Order*. New York: Simon & Schuster.

3. Gutmann, A. (2004). Unity and diversity in democratic multicultural education: Creative and destructive tensions. In J. A. Banks (Ed.), *Diversity and Citizenship Education: Global Perspectives* (pp. 71–96). San Francisco: Jossey-Bass.

4. Eurich, T. (2018). *Insight: The Surprising Truth About How Others See Us, How We See Ourselves, and Why the Answers Matter More Than We Think*. New York: Penguin Random House.

5. Cullen, Louis M. (2003). *A History of Japan, 1582–1941: Internal and External Worlds*. Cambridge: Cambridge University Press.

6. Mickes, John Wixted, and Laura. (2017) "Eyewitness memory is a lot more reliable than you think" *Scientific American*. Retrieved 27 September 2017.

7. Chan, Jason C. K., and Jessica A. LaPaglia (22 August 2011). "The dark side of testing memory: Repeated retrieval can enhance eyewitness suggestibility" *Journal of Experimental Psychology* 17(4), 418–432.

8. Balandier, G. (1968) *Daily Life in the Kingdom of the Congo*. New York: Pantheon Books, 49–50.

9. Evans, Richard J. (2000). *In Defense of History*. New York: W.W. Norton & Company.

10. Berger, S. (2007). "History and national identity: Why they should remain divorced" *History and Policy*. www.historyandpolicy.org/papers/policy-paper-66.html>. Accessed 24 October 2013.

11. Lévi-Strauss, Claude. (1962 [1966]). *La Pensée Sauvage/The Savage Mind (Nature of Human Society)*. London: Weidenfeld & Nicolson.

12. Freire, P. (1970/1997). *Pedagogy of the Oppressed*. London: Bloomsbury Academy.

13. Banks, J. A. (2002). *An Introduction to Multicultural Education* (3rd ed.). Boston: Allyn and Bacon.

14. Conal, F., and Salevouris, M. J. (2010). *The Methods and Skills of History: A Practical Guide*. Oxford: Wiley-Blackwell.

15. Storey, Kelleher, W. (2015). *Writing History: A Guide for Students* (5th ed.). Oxford University Press.

16. Pinker, Steven. (2002). *The Blank Slate: The Modern Denial of Human Nature*. New York: Penguin Group.

17. Miles, R. (2001). *Who Cooked. The Last Supper: The Women's History of the World*. New York: Three Rivers Press.

18. Banks, J. A. (2003). *Teaching Strategies for Ethnic Studies* (7th ed.). Boston: Allyn and Bacon.

19. Hughes, J. D. (2009). *An environmental history of the world: Humankind's role in the Community of Life*. London: Routledge.

20. Wagner, D. A. (2014). *The Marketing of Global Warming: A Repeated Measures Examination of the Effects of Cognitive Dissonance, Endorsement, and Information on Beliefs in a Social Cause*. Proquest Digital Dissertations: https://pqdtopen.proquest.com/doc/

21. Todorov, T. (1999). *The Conquest of America: The Question of the Other*. Norman: University of Oklahoma Press.

22. Takaki, R. (2008). *A Different Mirror: A History of Multicultural America*. Boston: Back Bay Books, Little, Brown and Company.

23. Ponting, C. (2007). *A New Green History of the World: The Environment and the Collapse of Great Civilizations*. New York: Vintage Books.

Chapter 6

Pedestal

Idolizing and Glorifying versus Demonizing and Deprecating ((Super)heroines and (Super) heroes, and Real Villains and Villainesses)

>Andrea: Unhappy is the land that breeds no hero.
>Galileo: No, Andrea: Unhappy is the land that needs a hero.
>
>—Bertolt Brecht, *Life of Galileo*
>(1938), Scene 12, p. 115

OVERVIEW

Pedestal is all about who is raised up and taught as heroic and who is downgraded to lesser status or marginalized in history and social science. In addition, there is discussion of people and places left out altogether who should be part of the story.

HEADLINE!

Suffrage Statue finally approved. Central Park will finally get a statue honoring historical women. Alejandra.occonnell2amny.com

I. INTRODUCTION

A definition to examine as we develop who makes history: "Pedestal . . . the base or support on which a statue, obelisk, or column is mounted. Also used in reference to a situation in which someone is greatly or uncritically admired."[1]

Deep within our species is a need to recognize and honor leadership. As nations and empires have grown ever more populous and complex, leaders have become historical characters in societies. The famous psychologist Jung argues that within our "collective unconscious" lies a need for both authority and liberty, creating a conflict within people about the kind of leadership they seek from family, friends, and government.[2]

Pedestals were inherited from the Greek Classical Age, when sculptures of people were placed on small Greek- and Roman-style pillars or blocs to connote their importance. We can learn about famous Greek and Roman figures from studying these sculptures. We can also get a better understanding of the imagery being used and the techniques for rendering such a figure.

Sculptures and statues raised on pedestals or mounted on blocs above us are still part of our culture though we may not pay much attention to ones we pass. In today's language, putting someone on a pedestal has several meanings that include a form of honor, raising a person up above the ordinary; creating a sense of worship for a person whose accomplishments are extraordinary, like our friends Napoleon or Washington or Sun Yat-Sen, or better yet mythic figures like Wonder Woman and Superman.[3]

Most ordinary people do not rate a sculpture in public, only the important and special receive this type of treatment. In most cultures, particularly those who celebrate heroines and heroes, create public images and regularly set up statues and busts of significant figures, particularly political and social heroines and heroes.[4]

Pedestals, the concept of raising up a figure in long-enduring stone, brass or iron, has lasted through thousands of years of history. We have a great deal more knowledge of the elite of the past than we do of the ordinary people largely because of the honor and obeisance performed in their favor. Placing leaders above us is a trait even in many democracies, certainly so in monarchies, dictatorships, and totalitarian regimes.

Thus, statues, busts, sculptures, and commemoration plaques frequently are used in history to recognize, honor, and celebrate accomplishments for the nation and its people. Given the current state of most world cultures, there is still a strong tendency to promote and remember men rather than women, especially men who served the country in leadership and military positions. This includes warriors and generals, political figures, and liberators, and sometimes ordinary people who performed heroic deeds for the state.

Even in ancient times, where there was a state, figures might appear in grandiose form. Even when we are not sure who or what they were, we get a sense of power, accomplishment and respect from their images that would not accrue to a regular citizen. How a person is portrayed, the symbols used often points to their status, strength, and success, for the culture, nation, and empire. Those on pedestals attest to developed historical traditions designed to create consciousness and sharing leader figures.[5]

Choosing people, leaders, to be honored and remembered, means that real and imagined founders and maintainers of a culture must be chosen from history and mythology to represent history. Many nations enjoy and recognize mythological figures more readily sometimes than real ones, and treasure them in special ways. These figures serve as "archetypes" for people to mimic and role-play, perhaps falling into literary "types," for example, king, warrior, magician, and lover.[6]

This is probably safer than raising up real people who, after all, may have faults, blemishes, and actions that upon close analysis do not qualify them as outstanding heroines or heroes. We do not care much for those with significant flaws. And imaginary cultural epic heroines and heroes are exempt from fake news because these are the ideals to measure real people against.[7]

Figure 6.1 **Marble Head of Zeus, Second Century AD.** Original in British Museum, image licensed to Wikipedia commons: public domain. Zeus, Jupiter, King of the Gods on a pedestal. Wikipedia/Roman marble colossal head of Zeus, second century AD (British Museum) CPU common license/public domain.

Mistakes and poor policies, or disapproved actions and behaviors may undo some toppling them from their historical high niche. In some cases, cultural shifts, changing mores and values may render those we once thought highly of as deeply suspect. At certain times in history, figures emerge to be honored for their conquests and defense of the country. But after 1877, and the creation of the Jim Crow era, once cherished characters like the lordly plantation owner, are later seen as overly violent, brutal conquerors, or defenders of a cultural elite.[8] These folks are now seen as unworthy of praise, much less of building expensive statues for, to set in parks.

There are ups and downs to the pedestal business. In some cases, there are clashing views, serious disagreements about who gets the marble treatment. The U.S. Civil War yielded numerous commemorative statues in both the North and South, mainly of generals and politicians, especially so in the period well after Reconstruction.

The South wished to keep its distinct character alive in memory and therefore honored confederates who fought the North, building statues in their memory and flying the confederate "stars and bars" flag, or singing favorite battle songs like "Dixie." Songs, symbols, and heroes (not many heroines, alas) keep the culture going, even though their side lost the war. But perhaps they won the war in spite of the losing the battle?

While specific people are honored on pedestals, others forgotten and/or marginalized. This is a function of government and culture, and while sometimes it reinforces differences rather than commonalities, it does demonstrate the power to name who shall sit atop the column. A few remain popular and recognizable across society and for long periods of history, but these are fairly rare.

However, as times change, and when questioning begins in many cultures, some of those raised up are reexamined and found wanting. Then the statuses and pedestals are knocked down. When change is in the wind, this revision of values happens both fallen statues, and new statues, represent cultural change and social evolution.

Pericles, a leading and famous citizen of Ancient Athens, was renowned for his oratory and served in leadership positions during time of crisis. The bust below would make a nice introduction to how leaders are portrayed, and you could learn a bit of Greek as well. Note the Athenian military helmet and the serious demeanor of the subject and his well-trimmed beard.

But is it really him or an idealized figure, smoothed over showing no warts or skin lines?

All of his head is stuck on a powerful chunk pedestal stone from 2,500 years ago, in 411 BCE. Is this statue designed for the home or the public and could it be considered propaganda? Is it impressive?

Research will reveal that Pericles was a superb speechmaker, and Thucydides, a noted historian of the time recorded the leader's most famous speech, "Funeral Oration" to honor those who died in battle. This speech still serves as a model for people honoring the war dead and promoting the benefits of citizenship and the statue also serves as a model for the portrayal of heroes in military style, generals, conquerors, kings, and democratic top office holders.[9]

The pedestal effect helps in promoting a leader's glorification and uplift her or him to heroic proportions, and may be followed and celebrated. In reality a character may have done untold damage to a nation's economy, political system, and population. Leadership may turn in the direction of power and privilege all the while spinning a myth about the public good or keeping good order.

How and why leaders are portrayed, like the bust of Pericles, can yield important clues to politics and culture of the times, and strikingly we almost always instinctively know when we are looking at the image of a leader. Even

Figure 6.2 Bust of Pericles, Famous Greek Leader and Orator. Pericles, Vatican Museum, circa 430 BCE, Museo PioClementino, #269 photographer Jastrow (2006) public domain. Bust of Pericles: with the inscription in Greek "Pericles, son of Xanthippus, Athenian." Marble Roman copy of a Greek original from c. 430 B.C.E. Vatican Museum, Museo Pio-Clementino, muses hall, Rome) #269, photographer. Jastrow (2006) public domain/Wikipedia.

a relatively unfamiliar sculpture from a distant culture can yield interpretations of leadership, though the pedestal is shaped differently.

Admiration and adoration produce a problem of "blindness" to faults by leaders, and especially in democracies (full or partial), causing citizens to be less wary of potential dangers and misconduct than they should. In many cases, part or most of the population desires the leader because the leader reflects their deep-seated prejudices and soothes their anxieties about "others" while reassuring people *about their important place in the world.*

The tendency to raise up and glorify leaders, from small groups to nations, to international acclaim, tends to build adrenalin rushes of admiration that blot out potential and real faults. The positives tend to overwhelm the negatives! But history's relentless drift and change holds surprises for those on pedestals as well as for ordinary citizens.

Teachers of social studies, social sciences, and history must keep the "pedestal" problem in mind when studying ANY leader, female or male, in history.[10] Review accomplishments before endorsing! Check out where the proposal for persons on pedestals originated, and who suggested it. Was there a design committee, a leader, a politico, a culture heroine? Consider who is missing from placement on a pedestal, marginalized from discussions, left out of the story and the honor.

This Olmec head from 3,000 years ago or so is huge, wider and taller than the average person by far, and placed on a pedestal or foundation. Many others were found all over Veracruz Province in Mexico. These are among the oldest sculptures dated in Mexico which has long, complex, and rich archeological history. The Olmecs are considered the oldest examples of a state entity or kingdom in the region, and many of their styles were copied by later peoples, the Mayans, Zapotecs, and Aztecs. Note the solidity and squareness and size. No one knows who this is actually but for teaching purposes it doesn't matter. Focus on the questions you will ask about leaders and pedestals, states and empires.

- What qualities is this giant head projecting?
- How does artist and leader want you to feel?
- Why are all facial features, eyes, lips, ears, and head so magnified?
- Why is the pose looking right at you?
- What is the sculpture saying about probable status?
- If you put all clues together, what conclusion would you draw about the culture he led?

A pedestal upon which rest a giant head, therefore, serves many purposes in a social order. It can be used to uplift a person, offer recognition, project a

Figure 6.3 San Lorenzo Colossal Olmec Head, Circa 1000 BCE, Veracruz, Mexico.
Wikipedia photograph, 2005–2006, GNU free documentation license.

sense of awe. Since this one is twice human size, it immediately calls attention by size as well as expression and style. The head is a very valuable piece of evidence and demands intense observation and careful interpretation.[11]

The statue allows members of the culture to remember a noted leader, and serve the interests of building a state. Leaders, especially founders of nations and people who assist in crises situations, are remembered because of their efforts in organizing survival, and building pride.

Pedestals offer honor to leaders in history, past and present, and tell us what sort of heroines and heroes continue to influence and build a culture's story about itself. Even if we don't know who the person was, a statue renders them noticed as outstanding, rather than ordinary. A statue is a signal or perhaps multiple signals about what and whom is important to a culture.

II. LEADERS AND FOLLOWERS

a. Do we need heroines and heroes?

Audience Popularity

Certain leaders who become part of the history of a state, for example, founding mothers and fathers, are particularly useful in creating and maintaining feelings of pride. A few leaders even gain international fame and recognition. The leader is often a striking figure who projects a sense of authority and power. As years pass, and positive actions are associated with the leader, her or his status begins to rise and a more powerful set of associations begins to develop. The pedestal is growing larger, longer, and recognition wider and deeper. A test, for instance, might be name and image recognition by a first grader, and by you, the reader.

As positives begin to expand and negatives become increasingly suppressed or overwhelmed by accomplishments, the leader takes on heroic qualities not attributed to her or him previously. The leader becomes a symbol, an icon, of the nation, its people, and culture, and perhaps gains superhuman qualities. This shift in valuation and affect symbolizes the beginning of a cult of personality with epic and heroic proportions. Faults are forgiven and forgotten.

The machinery of the state, its people, and the media assist in growing the sense of power and significance attributed to a great leader, past, present, and future. Statuses and busts arise and are distributed across the land leading to easy recognition of leader who has leadership qualities others must emulate. The shadow of a great leader can cover a land for a very longtime requiring newcomers and outsiders to adapt to her or his (real or imagined) accomplishment levels.

Heroes and heroines become beloved, cherished, and respected, not simply as very competent human beings, as good organizers and conquerors, or governors, but as icons of faith and loyalty. Superior qualities are alluded to great leaders who evolve into historical symbols of the culture across world mythology.[12] "Fathers" and a few "Mothers" of their nations often fall into this kind of worshipful devotion, such as Augustus, Napoleon, George Washington, and Nelson Mandela. Once in a while a "Mother" pops up such as Golda Meir, Catherine the Great of Russia, or Queen Zenobia leader of ancient Palmyra. Mothers tend to be treated differently and portrayed differently but once you seek examples, there are more than might be expected across global history.[13]

Let's take a look at a female figure from history: Catherine the Great of Russia. Her portrayal makes an interesting contrast to many of the male kings

Figure 6.4 **Portrait of Empress Catherine the Great of Russia, 1729–1796.** GNU free use license/Wikipedia, original Kunsthistorisches Museum. *Portrait of Queen Catherine II of Russia (1729–1796) an important person in history.* Date 1780s Medium oil on canvas Dimensions Height: 85.5 cm (33.6"); Width: 68 cm (26.7 Collection Accession number GG_7131 Object history Alter Kaiserlicher Besitz; Hofburg References described at wikidata, URL: https://www.khm.at/de/object/be1df9a5d0/Source/Photographer Kunsthistorisches Museum. This work is in the public domain in its country of origin. Deutsch: Abgebildete Person: Kaiserin Katharina II. v. Russland, Tochter v. C.A. Anhalt-Zerb

and emperors. She is elaborately dressed projecting a sense of high status, being well-dressed with an elaborate hairdo, magnificent tiara and necklace, and an ermine gown. Catherine has a sweet smile and inviting expression that draws the viewer in rather than repelling them.

The tzarina (who was born in Prussia and married to the tzar at a youthful princess) comes off as important yet approachable. How many other details might you notice and what kind of overall interpretation could you develop about Catherine in comparison to Pericles or to the Olmec leader? Who seems to project greatest accessibility, who least, and why? Her story is quite complex and interesting and she was very politically astute at court politics deposing her husband, the tzar, in a palace coup, belying the kindly look in the portrait.

Reflected Identity

Leaders are regularly needed to conduct and direct a people, a nation, into a better, more prosperous, and engaging future. But heroines/heroes are needed to lead people to greatness, to a better life, to a place of political and cultural dominance over many other peoples and nations. Such leaders may take on the status of superheroines/heroes much like those reflected in cartoon and film characters.

The heads of state, or culture figures that are most recognizable, offer many sympathetic and sometimes aggressive qualities that may appeal at a certain point in history. This appeal attracts audiences, voters, citizens, supporters, in all forms of government and artistic leadership. Dictators and monarchs and presidents as well must project an identity that the mass of people, at least a majority, feel represents their tribe, community, and nation in the world.[14]

Disidentification, disorientation, and the loss of identity, and a decline of values can have terrifying and destructive effects on a society. Conflicts that were soothed over may come to the fore, protests break out, and groups attack each other. Social cohesion is built partly be leaders in government and other fields attracting participation and rewarding people for joining in a community enterprise. Most view the leader's job as keeping a state together building a group and national identity that will mobilize against outside and inside threats.

In effect, elites socialize ordinary citizens and noncitizens into ways of doing things that fit the culture to which they belong. Everyone, foreign born or native, begins to share a common identity and common values that make for a more harmonious and happy social order, a commonality of concerns and habits. Persecuting portions of a society, or creating groups of second-class citizens whether because of race, gender, culture or subculture, nearly always leads to strengthening biases and promoting internal conflicts.

The people, citizens, and immigrants, may absorb the leader's reflected identity, growing into a common political culture. "Reflected Identity" works both ways: the leadership provides the character and behavior that draws in an audience who voluntarily recreate themselves to match the culture and values of a leader and her or his administration.[15] Founding mothers and fathers, reigning and elected officeholders help everyone build a new culture from the old, adapting traditions to new circumstances.

For example, Mustafa Kemal Ataturk, Founding Father of the Republic of Turkey created a new government (1923–1938) separating church and state in Turkey while building democratic institutions. Most of the population went along identifying with the new leader because their previous collapse after World War I was pretty much a disaster so many enthusiastically adopted the new Westernized culture.

Sun Yat-Sen performed a similar service for China, and Jomo Kenyatta for Kenya. Sun worked to modernize China after the fall of the imperial dynasty and monarchy, while Kenyatta led a rebellion against British colonial rule, eventually establishing a republic in Kenya. Periods of conflict with colonial masters and foreign powers were followed by a more harmonious set of social relations in many colonized places centered on fusing groups into a relatively united people with their own nation-state.

Lifestyles and Charisma

A new leadership and elite, as well as culture heroines and heroes, also project a new sense of style and purpose. This may extend to new styles of dress, new forms of music and art, and literary creations that reflect changing values. Fiction, music, and art also take on new styles and meaning, sometimes providing superheroines and heroes that mimic the political and economic shifts in the culture.

Even cartoon characters may be created that offer important messages, and a sense of identity to people, even though invented. The cartoon and literary characters, Wonder Woman, Superman, Zorro, and others, reflect issues that need solving in a society, missed gender or racial or ethnic populations in need of widely appreciated culture heroines and heroes. For example, entertainment and literature may seriously lack representatives from and for many subcultures.

Where are TV or Internet programs in the United States with stars of indigenous origins, Latino heritage, or female business tycoons or warriors? Where are Israeli culture stars of Ethiopian, Yemenite, or Moroccan origin? Where are Algerians, Tunisians, and other Levantines represented in French theater and cinema? Where are Pakistani and Indian detectives in British mystery series?

Every segment of a population needs someone to represent their lifestyles and cultures with the larger common culture?

Fiction may reinforce fact, and fact reverberates to the advantage of very powerful and charismatic leaders who approach and reach a very high pedestal indeed. Ever better images are possible if the leader or her/his party and followers control every branch of government, or exercise strong influence and control over the broadcast media.

In teaching history, those leaders who approach the highest status and levels of affection should probably be accorded the strongest levels of suspicion, calling for reviews of their accomplishments and policy decisions, and perhaps their personalities as well. These representatives might be token assimilationists. You might inquire how close the story has come to myth and legend.

While many American presidents are nearly forgotten, several have names and images enshrined in culture and history. In the United States, Washington, Lincoln, and the Roosevelts, live on and can be recognized by nearly all citizens. They become symbols of the state and its traditions, promoting admiration and identification with their accomplishments on behalf of the common good. Others fall by the wayside. But the list of symbols tends to heavily emphasize the ruling class in most places.

Nearly all societies and nations have their historical symbols and leaders, but our society may be unaware of who gets the top ratings and why. Every culture, or nearly so, recognizes historical traditions and places certain famous people on pedestals, in textbooks, as statues in the park, and across schools. Their portraits become quite familiar and they are seen as important parts of the national story. We need to think about the reasons behind popularity and worship, affection and status.

In many cases, leaders don't necessarily have to be political to become culture heroines and heroes. Many come from the arts, music, social movements, science, and labor and finance and are quickly recognized though perhaps not to the extent of the movers and shakers of government and empire, sports and athletics, art and music and literature. For example, Albert Einstein is probably more widely recognized than two-thirds of the world's leaders.

Most portrayals are positive in style, content, and language, with leaders portrayed as more than ordinary people, though a few remain attached to their humble origins. Sometimes the imagery gets out of hand as the statues and praises reach epic proportions. Symbols and signs of nationhood, like flags, flowers, birds, and animals, often accompany political leaders.

3. Moral Symbols and Entertainment Values

Moral values build identity with a people bound together by great women and men, as well as territorial boundaries and shared values and laws.

However, just as there are great leaders, there are also villainesses and villains, who are downgraded and vilified to a degree that obscures their accomplishments and the reasons for the rise to power. Here too, like the heroic, we easily lose track of how they came to power or notoriety, and they are now clearly seen in a negative light.

People have a fairly short historical memory, alas. And they tend to skip research into why and how judgments of greatness and power developed. We tend to remember those heroines/heroes taught in school or celebrated by the state in some form, forgetting or skipping over many "lesser" rather skillful and impressive leaders and villains.

It is very easy to have a warm and friendly discussion of George Washington, but it is very difficult to have an unemotional analysis of Hitler's career, for example, or understand the fall of the Weimar Republic in Germany. Our emotions get in the way, especially when we choose figures who were rebellious, oppressed, or aggressive like some of our famous indigenous leaders, for example, Chief Brandt, Geronimo, Sitting Bull, and Crazy Horse.

How we choose which leaders to honor or vilify depends a lot on their accomplishments, and how these are viewed across time periods. Leaders' reputations are constantly revised and judged from different times and places, with different values and results. We need figures who fill in the story left open by a distinct dearth of social reformers, indigenous peoples, women and LGBT representatives, intellectuals, musicians, artists and writers, and so forth.

One time period may honor leaders from wartimes, others leaders from peacetime. One of the big issues in discussing leaders and leadership in any field is that they become icons of a time and place, unassailable figures of greatness or horror making them so difficult to approach. Portrayals glorify famous people to such a positive or negative extent that we view them uncritically.

Most leaders are actually human beings just like us, well almost, and their story upon researching it is a mixed bag of ups and downs, accomplishments and bad decisions. They also hold great powers and/or high status, and we rarely hear about their problems. Exemplary leaders build a nation giving it culture and historical heroines/heroes, but not real people who lived inside history. They can communicate to us through their own speeches, writings, and images.[16]

We must wait a bit to decide on a level of admiration, studying until a good deal of evidence is amassed and evaluated.

Examining leaders, good and evil and in-between, female and male, through their own actions and writings as well as by their praise singers and court historians. This doesn't mean that praise is withheld, rather that the praise or blame is based on evidence of actions and interpretations that can be defended with facts and reasons. All of this data helps us develop or assign (tentative) scores of our own for those we follow.

Teaching history and social science, particularly with respect to "famous" people, whether held in awe or horror, especially with regard to "leaders" is inherently dangerous. Be suspicious of quick judgments! Discussion and evaluation of leaders requires discipline and neutrality at least to start. Just how we view history depends a great deal on the way historians and other leaders have influenced our thinking about the people we study up to and including present-day leaders.

Our judgments arise from our own moral compass influenced by a complex set of social, religious, political, and ethical values, those we hold dearest. Studying history especially heroines and heroes, villains, and villainesses, test our values, and ourselves, our commitments and helps build a code to live by. This an exciting but not easy task.

By leaders we are including women and men, culture figures, cult figures, sports names, intellectuals, historical and political founders, and present-day figures "idolized" or "popularized" in media. In other words, we are including the entire elite built by national, and international study and supported by media identification and dissemination. This elite, some kind of elite, has probably existed in most places across recorded history.

As soon as "the Leader" or the "Famous Person" is trotted out in some form, our first rule as good historians is to be suspicious! We must NOT accept everything conveyed to us about either existing, developing, or potential celebrity. The greater the fame perhaps, the more skeptical students and teachers should be, and the more cross-checking we accomplish on words and deeds the better, before agreeing or disagreeing with ratings.[17]

We need to carefully examine the portrayal of the rich, powerful, famous, and popular in words, pictures, sound, and film, without any commitment of belief, or of disbelief. Let's just pretend that we are from Mars or Venus and newly acquainted with human communications about outstanding and infamous characters from the annals of local, national, and global history. Let's zero in on words and their use, particularly words that strongly convey warm or cold feelings about an historical character including the downtrodden and disinherited.

III. BECOMING VISIBLE

Becoming visible is a difficult task. Being visible over a long time period is even more difficult. Growing into an icon is exceedingly rare but often expresses great power as a symbol.

a. Visible and Invisible

Who is visible in a social order and who invisible is set by class status and gender and race throughout history.

High status and wide recognition are accorded to only a few people in any society. The pedestal treatment is fairly rare. Status is usually driven by governments and by publicity in both ancient and modern cultures. Motives for honor and fame are usually politically motivated.[18]

Some figures achieve and are awarded status for political reasons, and others due to celebrity, intellectual, or artistic popularity, and/or prowess in the military. For most people, becoming visible at all, to all, is a huge task even where and when there is often considerable popularity given to an individual. Much depends on recognition by the state or media.

For others, even where there is a record of outstanding achievement, recognition can be halting, partial, and evanescent. People fade from public notice easily in a large society and that perhaps may be for the best, but it does narrow the field by diminishing selection. A brief bout of fame may be better than none of course, but lasting fame is for the few.

Many members of a society receive family, local, and job recognition, mostly fleeting, though heartwarming to the recipients at the time. Below this group are the many who live quiet, ordinary lives seldom finding their stories in history and journalistic publications. Once in a while, the press decides to feature ordinary citizens in news articles, public reports, or interview on TV or radio or Internet.

Below this level, most people's lives are taken up in pursuit of making a living, keeping ahead of their bills, but some people fall onto hard times they cannot easily resolve. Few are recognized and most are marginalized or unmentioned. The lower the status the less the chance of achieving a pedestal or any kind of recognition. Most remain invisible.[19]

Status is a huge problem in history since most ordinary and lower status people, for example, slaves, the poverty stricken, peasants, and country folk leave little or no records behind. Neither are they accorded much attention by most historians or higher levels of society. They are visible only when social change happens on a big scale and legal and political status is overturned in a rebellion or revolution or war.

Those who rebel and destroy, attacking the ruling elite may be remembered if they win, but suppressed if they lose. Many a leader has vanished from history, erased. Therefore, some of the most interesting events in history are social upheavals like revolutions and wars, when we get to notice the lower classes and masses for the first time. It is almost like a revelation of the lives of majorities in most societies.

b. Celebrated and Suppressed

Which members of a society are celebrated, marginalized, and which suppressed, is strongly related to their social status, sex, race, and role. Those especially celebrated usually reflect the central values epitomized by the elite class of society, the upper class or military power.

Celebration is arranged by the elite for its outstanding citizens through many means: holidays, statues, media, posters, official history, and textbooks.[20] A court surrounds their accomplishments, victories, and escapades, weaving them into historical records of the country. Years and years of honors and media representation produce widespread recognition and the individual becomes part of a nation's shared story. The citizens bask in the reflected glory of their fellow citizen, who is growing larger and larger in both reality and imagination.

Rebellious, critical, and revolutionary figures, of whatever gender or race, are usually, but not always, left out of the central narrative of the state. Long histories of nations and peoples often produce stories of founding mothers and fathers, but these may evolve over time, with more recent accruals to the famous, with many figures added over the centuries. Politics may shift with the times, from left to right to center. Each shift may produce new characters considered for pedestals, as well as causing older figures to be reassessed.

Changing times, particularly during periods of economic innovation, social conflict, reform movements, and revolutions may alter who is seen as heroic or villainous. New folks arise and others fall, some rise very high, others fall below recognition. Some revaluations lead to total demotion and hostility. In some cases, what might be seen as positive change by some is viewed with hostility by others. Columbus, for example, is in danger of losing his pedestal because of revised thinking about his treatment of indigenous people, formerly called Native Americans.

Italians, on the other hand, see Columbus as "theirs" and as a culture hero. They march on Columbus Day for recognition and to keep a tradition alive while Indigenous People's Day is celebrated by Native Americans and others trying to right the wrongs of historical visibility and invisibility. Where this will all come out decades from now is hard to say since there is competition between two powerful lobbying groups with their own leadership.

In some cases, the powers-that-be, the elite, attempt to erase people entirely out of the story. These attempts to suppress portions and characters in a story can make great social studies lessons, demonstrating biases as well as the power of states and leaders to edit and/or eliminate portions of history.

High office allows the power to both write and rewrite history, eliminating those parts that are critical, embarrassing, or shameful in favor of a much better story of faith and heroism. In some administrations, the story changes every day, with contradictions of the original replacing other contradictory tales, leaving everyone confused. In a few instances that we know about, figures, even important figures, have literally been erased from the[21] picture.[22]

In the Soviet Union under Joseph Stalin, leaders were often "purged," sent to exile or murdered when there were differences of opinion, rivalries, or plots. Stalin was reputedly paranoid and watchful about keeping full control of the government and suspicious of possible plotters. In many cases, the suspects were high-ranking ministers and diplomats. Their records and their images were often expunged entirely from the historical record, after exile and before death.[23, 24]

Persons, even groups, can be erased from history, and many are missing today, many we only know about because there are corroborating accounts and pictures.[25] In the documented picture below, the same photograph of Lenin speaking in Moscow during the revolution shows two other leaders to the right side. These two, Trotsky and Kamenev, were outstanding members of the Bolsheviks, but later came under suspicion by Stalin, who had them literally erased from the photograph, and textbooks reprinted with them missing. Note the doctoring of the photo, not such a good job since the forger lightened and blurred the picture to achieve the goal of removal.

How might you present this and other photographs for analysis?

What themes could be developed: forgery, doctoring images, shifting values and leadership?

Modern technology has actually made it easier to erase, doctor, rearrange, and destroy or edit accounts, change photographs, and hack electronic records. Nearly every computer savvy schoolchild around the globe who has mastered cutting and pasting can change photos at will, making a figure look silly, evil, or noble, as desired. Usually the goal is to satirize or make someone look goofy, but think of the possibilities for damage if we remain unaware. Faking news or views or doctoring photos is now as easy as can be even for ordinary hackers.[26]

Celebrity is not a guarantee of escape from satire or attack. Conflicting political policies can get a figure demoted and diminished. Media can lose interest and the figure fades from our view. As vast quantities of new images, news, views, studies, reports, bickering, and clashing flow into our minds and veins from the Internet and TV and films and YouTube.com and email and texting, we begin to refocus on the present and the past slips out of our grasp unless you know where to look. Maybe this is suppression by inundation rather than vengeance and burial?

Nevertheless, being suspicious of grand accounts and looking for alternatives from the oppressed and downtrodden, the suppressed and exiled, can stimulate provocative questions about history and its sources. Confusion and

Figure 6.5   Lenin Giving a Revolutionary Speech in Sverdlov Square, Moscow, 1919.
Trotsky and Kamenev in foreground erased by Stalin from later photo reprints/photo submitted to Wikipedia for free use in 2018. Lenin gives his famous speech to Soviet troops in Moscow: in the foreground were his fellow leaders Leon Trotsky and Lev Kamenev. Lenin giving a revolutionary speech in Sverdlov Square in Moscow in 1919 (Grigory Goldstein [1870–1940] own work). During Stalin's rise to power, he disliked both rivals and had them deleted from the photograph, editing them out of the picture. Photo submitted to Wikipedia in 2018.

contradiction in stories and histories is the best invitation for historical detectives to try out their sleuthing skills. Both the celebrated and the suppressed have left us interesting stories to make use of in understanding historical evolution and change.

c. Central and Marginal

Characters real and imagined can be central to the history of a nation or people, or even the entire planet. Centrality means that these people have become an honored and celebrated figure in local, national, and international history. It is relatively easy to tell when a person has become central to history by how many people recognize and relate to their image or story. Knowing a character's story is more than just a compliment, it is a show of support, a sharing of loyalty, and an expression of approval.

Feeling that a character is central to the story is a demonstration of knowledge and positive feeling. It implies an emotional connection, real affection, not simply a fact to know. These feelings of loyalty can be utilized by elites working to retain power in the here and now. Feelings can also be twisted every which way to support everything from fascism to revolution. All nations have adopted the same kinds of symbols as expressions of loyalty and service: flags, songs, stories, characters (leaders), values and beliefs, and customs. A specific set of these symbols and personalities is presented as uniquely their own, central to national or imperial identity.

To challenge these symbols and signs, values and elites, is to risk conflict and perhaps oblivion for the counter-story being promoted. It is very, very difficult to challenge a story that is central to the myth and reality of a people. And it may also be a dangerous challenge, resulting in criticism, suppression and even exile or containment. Who might criticize Mahatma Gandhi in India, Mao Zedong in China, or Abraham Lincoln in the United States? As a leader or culture hero gets closer to becoming central, there is less ability to revise their history.

By contrast, those who are marginalized, meaning pushed out of the center to the periphery of the story, are far easier to criticize and to forget. National histories tend to be subservient to positive stories about all the good parts of their tale, like becoming wealthy, but overlooks most of the bad and embarrassing parts, like imperialism condoning land grabs. National leaders reinforce central figures, central stories, and central values day after day, decade after decade so we all recognize the founders, the symbols, and the beliefs that should be endorsed.

Most societies tend to reinforce the national or imperial story, expanding recognition of established figures, while dismissing, sidelining, and eliminating the marginals. While central figures reflect the dominant majority or largest and most successful minority, the marginals usually represent "others"; other racial and ethnic groups, less successful minorities, workers and peasants, and the impoverished of all races. Portions of any population contain an elite, an upwardly rising professional class, a middle, and a downtrodden proletariat. There may also be sizeable pockets of noncitizens and non-natives who may be tolerated or discriminated against.

Margins radiate out from the center in cascading rings, each representing greater distance from the center of wealth and power. The rich and famous, the talented and popular are almost always upfront in history, while the lesser souls are barely recognized unless there is a huge uprising or a general draft for the army, navy, and air force. Far out into the solar system of rings are large numbers of nameless and faceless folk.

In teaching history, and in learning history, there is always a problem in getting the whole picture of a people, one that includes and acknowledges the role of greater and lesser mortals in maintaining the culture. Most of what we pay attention to as teachers, and in history textbooks, deals with the classes rather than the masses.

Most of what we give time to deals with males rather than females, and certainly just a tiny bit about other sexual orientations if these are even mentioned. Most characters in history, both fictional and factual, are members of the educated, rich, and powerful upper classes. *We barely* talk about peasants unless they revolt, and then we view them with fear and suspicion.

There were millions of slaves in the United States and throughout great swaths of time and territory, but they are marginal to most stories. Once in a while we get the firsthand story or even secondhand story of a slave: these are so rare as to be treasured because we find out what the outsiders and marginals felt and experienced in history. Thus, Frederick Douglass and Olaudah Equiano have provided literary treasure that give insight into stories usually left out of the greater narrative. The story of Spartacus in Rome, and Wat Tyler in England both written by historians yields powerful accounts of the downtrodden rising up against the rulers of the time.

Always ask who is doing the work in a social system and where they came from, then see what secrets you discover about the hidden marginals.

d. Repressed (Ignored?) and Reclaimed

Segments of society are often overlooked or ignored. Others want their pedestals in place but are repressed perhaps due to loss of interest, or due to changing social values, or purposeful political interference. Entire peoples and their culture heroines/heroes may be available for visiting and viewing but remain relatively or totally unknown to most of the populace.

In some cases, monuments and histories are easily found in these days of Internet searches, but not in the public limelight. As noted previously, the Internet is a wonderful invention but a teacher or student has to know what to look for and then decide how to present it in class. Search engines can dig up a huge number of examples, but many sources are simply information-oriented and lack plans for classroom presentation. Even where there are superb resources, these may be relatively obscure or demand considerable work to employ.

Ignored peoples, and events is probably the largest category for those left out of most national stories. Figures, histories, social science studies are all out there but only touch now and then, few "hits" as they say, in comparison to national icons. This is likely in almost every large national society, with elites and political leadership grabbing most of the attention.

Ethnic and racial groups usually have long-standing complaints about their reduced roles in dominant narratives.

A fine example of this off-hand approach is the treatment of indigenous peoples in American history or Canadian history. Crazy Horse, considered a hero to the Plains peoples, particularly the Sioux, is the subject of a huge monument to reclaim his place in history. This is located in the Black Hills of South Dakota, developed as a counter-pedestal to the very famous Presidents' Monument at Mount Rushmore that is a major tourist attraction. Crazy Horse's is not far from the Presidents', one of whom was crucial to the defeat of the Sioux Nation in U.S. history.

Look it up.

Indigenous peoples in Canada have a similar invisibility problem, and also often protest their treatment. Lack of attention as central also plagues the story of Louis Riel, a mixed-race leader of people called Metis (which means mixed in French), descended from Canadian indigenous peoples who married French trappers and explorers and formed a community of their own. Louis led the Northwest Rebellion in Canada in 1885 supported by a group of fighters against the Canadian militia in Saskatchewan over abuse of civil rights. It's a good story for the classroom and brings up many issues about who rates a pedestal.

Look this up, too.

Americans on the whole know even less about Canada and its record of repression and reclamation of pedestal candidates, and much less about Canadian native peoples than they do about U.S. groups. Invisibility and marginality can be found in every society, even those that have democratic histories.

African Americans have perhaps the best recognition in the United States because of an active civil rights movement, the revelations about slavery and Jim Crow institutions, and the Civil Rights movement. Many African Americans are represented in Congress and one has been president. Thus, they have access to quite a few heroine and hero pedestals and make frequent use of their heritage of outstanding historical figures, past and present. Other peoples, Latinos, Pacific Islanders, Asians, all part of the U.S. population, are less well treated and appear quite infrequently in media, textbooks, and general histories of the country's immigration story.

Gender is as usual a major issue, with far fewer women appearing in local, national, or global histories than men. Even fewer minority women appear in school textbooks. We know a few international and historical women who have made it to a pedestal, but we know very little and teach less about outstanding women in other nations and in global organizations.

So, as a general rule teachers and students can look for documents and images that are from marginalized communities the first and largest of which is: women! As half or more of the population since time began, female figures are in a distinct minority even after the women's liberation movement of the 1960s and 1970s and the rise of feminism and the expansion of educational opportunities. A recent study of state and local social studies requirements conducted by the federally funded Smithsonian Institution in 2017 showed a combined total of 737 historic figures mandated for textbook coverage. Of these figures, 559 were men, and 178 were women.[27]

Therefore, throughout history, across the globe, each and every society, has a series of in-groups and out-groups that help to determine how successful each will be at "becoming visible," remaining marginal, or staying invisible.

Red paint covered a statue of Christopher Columbus on Monday, October 14, 2019, in Providence, Rhode Island, after it was vandalized on the day named to honor him as one of the first Europeans to reach the New World. The statue has been the target of vandals on Columbus Day in the past.

IV. PEOPLE LIKE ME ON A PEDESTAL: RECOGNITION AND REPRESENTATION

A big question in teaching and learning history is whether pedestals are important and necessary, or can they be modified to accommodate those who feel marginalized, left out, or rejected.[28] Historical pedestals tend to be reserved for the relatively few heroes and fewer heroines. As society across the globe (with a few possible exceptions) seem to need figures to celebrate and honor, can we supply figures that will satisfy citizens?

a. Compliance and Complaint

Most people go along with authority, honoring and celebrating those chosen for placement at the center of socialization: leaders, culture figures, contributors to social progress, and responders to crises and attacks. Most people

Figure 6.6 Christopher Columbus Statue Vandalized in Providence, Rhode Island on Columbus Day 2019. Michelle R. Smith/AP News/www.nydailynews.com. Christopher Columbus statues vandalized in Providence, other U.S. cities. The Providence statue has been the target of vandals on Columbus Day in the past.

absorb patriotic feelings their leaders and the characters deemed worthy of honor in their society. People are socialized into a national or imperial culture of foods, symbols, leaders, famous citizens, and patriotic pride.

Respect and affection can be heartwarming and induce pride for in local, state, national, and even international figures. The founding fathers and mothers are adopted and feted, and used as markers for traditions and beliefs, like quoting James Madison or Thomas Jefferson's principles as guides to present-day behavior. On a global level, guidelines for ethical beliefs can be drawn from ancient faiths, Moses, Jesus, Mohammed, or from modern leaders like Gandhi, Martin Luther King Jr., and Nelson Mandela.

Positive feelings for leaders, faiths, democratic principles, and benevolent monarchs can help keep peace, grow affection for inclusive philosophies, and build shared values. The greater the potential for ideas and loyalties to cross borders and groups, the less negative the attitude toward others. Sharing, a sense of going along, compliance, can function as a uniting force across class, gender, race, and ethnicity. But this must be accompanied by genuine attention to the problems and needs of the downtrodden and poverty stricken, and to those groups that have been formerly invisible or marginalized.[29]

Conversely, if compliance is forced on everyone in a society by the dominant group who sees only their identity as defining the center, then complaints will develop and spread. Protests will evolve and explode the greater sense of inequality and repression. As social orders divide into two or more groups competing for the power to define identity and set values, the greater the chance for confusion, anger, dissatisfaction, and disaffection. Protests may begin, rebellions break out, politics divide, and opportunities for compromise diminish.

Complaint is a fundamental part of any complex society and it can be costly if it spreads widely in any part, subpart, or segment of a society. Compliance, willing compromise, cannot take place unless the demands and requests of the complainers are taken seriously from the center to the margins. Who, which leaders, occupy the pedestal in any culture or society at the time must try to deal with all segments of the population. Narrow, and narrowing, definitions of who is whom, who counts, especially who is "us" and who is "them" can give rise to prejudiced and biased worldviews rather than inclusive and open world views.

The big problem presented by narrow views of others, and the world, is that globalization has already taken its toll on identity, culture, and economics. The world is already well on its way to homogenization, a process that began with the birth of the first city and state. Unique cultures hardly exist anymore and those that do are in harm's way, suffering destruction, displacement, and dissolution.

We need a series of solutions that embrace more and wider groups of citizens who get to sit on pedestals, at least temporarily and get looked at by the populace as a whole.

b. Ordinary Heroines and Heroes

One solution proposed to humanize and reduce the size of pedestals, bringing them nearer to earth, is to extend the definition of heroism to ordinary people.

Rethink not only significant people in different fields, but also ordinary people, as having the potential to be witnessed, honored, and applauded for their actions. These can be people who responded to crises, floods, terrorism, bombings, charitable work, scientific and medical problems. In teaching history, why is so much space and time devoted to wars, conflict, and top leaders, and so little to the work and accomplishments of ordinary people?

For example, many suggested that the "first responders" to the falling of the World Trade Towers on September 11, 2001, the police, firemen, and others who tried to save people from the collapsing buildings, should be on pedestals. In fact, the memorial to September 11, 2001 in New York as well as the museum of the story and its wreckage invites tourists and visitors to engage with the evidence, learn the facts, and develop their own reinterpretations of the meaning of heroic action.

Throughout history, ordinary people have exerted leadership and heroism in many walks of life. There are categories of the heroic, military, civic, and social. Service to a country or empire may be regarded as a sacrifice to guarantee the safety of others. Of course, this may get out of hand and turn villainy if soldiers get out of hand and attack civilians or follow the orders of authority without thinking, or invade and destroy other peoples for motives of greed and power.

The most obvious ordinary heroines/heroes are those who officially (military, police, firemen, doctors, nurses, etc.) or unofficially serve to protect a society from external harm. There are also civil heroines and heroes who guarantee safety and well-being within a society protecting citizens from internal attacks, from crime, from illness, and from financial ruin. Of course, women as well as men can be part of the pattern of protection, and even children. Action motivated by deeply held values is part and parcel of heroic action.

Roles can cover a wide range from philanthropists and clergy, to charities medical services, and schools to guards, police, and military organizations. Civilians can rise to heroic heights during political and social crises, attacks, rebellions, invasions, and warfare, to natural catastrophes like floods, power failures, storms, and earthquakes.

There are ample opportunities for ordinary people to save and protect others from harm, and our value system usually extends gratitude and honor to those who aid their fellow human beings during stressful and dangerous situations. In fact, honors to the ordinary are often quite brief and personal while honors to the elite are extensive, costly, and long-lasting.

Once in a while ordinary people rate a statue, a museum, a celebration or perhaps a reward. A very few become the stuff of myth and legend. Doctors without Borders is an example of a civil worldwide organization seeking to aid people in dangerous places or where diseases are rampant. The doctors are all volunteers and are risking their lives to offer aid to the downtrodden.

The ordinary often become extraordinary during crises, but crises are (fortunately) relatively rare. Most of the ordinary heroines/heroes that we celebrate or recognize aid society by fulfilling the roles they have chosen professionally, as well as by roles they acquire. Many jobs can be viewed as providing succor to others, most prominently doctors, nurses, and ambulance teams. Their very jobs place them in the position of serving society, and their local neighborhoods, to prevent accidents, save lives by providing rapid assistance to those who are ill or in need.

Others take upon themselves duties that may include becoming active in reform movements, whistleblowers within corrupt organizations, and charitable endeavors to help a wide range of people: the homeless, the elderly, school children, or the impoverished. There are legions of heroic people in history who have volunteered to combat the problems of the day by pressuring for reform and control of a wide range of issues such as gun use, alcoholism, childcare, crime, child labor, mental health, and saving the environment.

U.S. history is replete with social reformers who have taken upon themselves the task of working to solve a problem or issue they see are deeply harmful. Nearly every society has a variety of deep-seated problems to solve and some extraordinary people are motivated to deal with it despite putting themselves at risk.

If not for ordinary heroines/heroes, society would function far less effectively and certainly less caringly.

c. Downtrodden and Disinherited

A second solution to the issue of who sits on a pedestal is to extend sympathy and recognition to those who have been underprivileged, downtrodden, and disinherited. This is a problematical category but does shine a light on those who have been assigned to lower castes and invisible roles in history. Authorities still do not particularly enjoy reviewing slave stories, the institution of slaver, and certainly not rebellious slaves! Too scary!

The downtrodden includes those captured into slavery, assigned to prisons, deprived of work, and relegated to the slums of societies. The disinherited includes those dispossessed of land, liberty, and property by conflict and invasion, some cases due to defeat and capture, others due to environmental collapse and/or economic changes. The groups overlap at least in part, but both paths lead to a significant loss of liberty, and degradation to the most difficult, demanding, and lowest paid or unpaid labor.

The poorest and most excluded segments of society are often the least recognized and almost never have one of their number placed on a pedestal. History tends to ignore the lower levels of the social order for a variety of complex reasons. In some cultures, there is an active dislike of the unsuccessful and impoverished; in others the poor are ignored and have to fend for themselves. Those who were at the bottom of the social order, like the "scheduled castes" in India, formerly and incorrectly nicknames "untouchables" were downtrodden because they originally did distasteful jobs like butchering and tanning livestock, a task forbidden by Hindu tradition.

Slaves in ancient Rome were often prisoners of war, and they seldom produced written accounts of their lives. But they can be studied through others' narratives (be suspicious!). A most famous case in film, story, and TV is Spartacus, who led a significant but ultimately defeated rebellion against the Roman Republic. Throughout history, slaves, peasants, serfs, whatever the label, tend to be purposely or inadvertently overlooked by those around them. They were expected to work away without attracting any attention, to remain invisible.

Rebellions and revolts by the downtrodden have been recorded a number of times in history, and make interesting, even gripping, reading though we are mostly missing original accounts from the leaders or participants. Most accounts come from the court historians and supporters of the authorities of the time. Interesting rebellions include Spartacus against Rome, the Jewish zealots against Rome, the Albigensian Heresy and the Wat Tyler rebellion of 1381 in medieval times, the Haitian revolution, and the Nat Turner revolt in the antebellum U.S. South. We have some original sources from the American South because runaway slaves were taught to read and write or learned to do so on their own, thus we have a few terrific primary sources.

The German peasant's War of is seldom taught, but a fascinating tale, as peasant groups began to attack those high pedestals, knights and barons. Women took the reins of power on occasion and attacked the nobles as well, while also forcing husbands into submission. Women of the medieval period through the Renaissance and beyond generally were invisible, had low status, and may be considered nearly slaves.

Interestingly, the famous cleric Martin Luther published a book condemning the rebellion with the title of "*Against the Murderous, Thieving Hordes of Peasants* in 1525. So much for their status. This could develop in a great lesson for keen observers and historical detectives. Note the important looking bearded knight in armor decorated with feathers and garlands. He is surrounded by peasants wearing tunics, caps, and crudely made shoes. The one in front is threatening the knight with a pitchfork and the rest seem armed as well with spears, rakes, and swords. They don't seem intimidated by his lordship and their banner is an unraveling shoe.

Certainly, women, the other half of every society, were very seldom in control of their own stories, but we do have husbands' and literary accounts that provide deep insight into women's lives. One of the major poets of the time left us a disturbing picture of peasant women's problems (and men as well) in a poem titled "Piers Plowman" written around 1370–1390 by an Englishman and there are several versions just to make things historically interesting in terms of provenance.

Figure 6.7 Lithography of the Great Peasants' Revolt in Germany, 1524–1525. Photographed and submitted to Wikipedia commons by Mr. I. Rosensweig for public use, Lizenstatis: public domain. A lithograph from the Great Peasants' Revolt in 1524–1525. Note pitchfork attack on noble (2004), photographed and submitted by Mr. Rozensweig for public use. Original from 1539, in German (Lizenzstatus: Public Domain. Quell eselbst gescannt).

> Burdened with children and landlords' rent;
> What they can put aside from what they make spinning they spend on housing,
> Also on milk and meal to make porridge with
> To sate their children who cry out for food
> And they themselves also suffer much hunger,
> And woe in wintertime, and waking up nights
> To rise on the bedside to rock the cradle,
> Also to card and comb wool, to patch and to wash,
> To rub flax and reel yarn and to peel rushes
> That it is pity to describe or show in rhyme
> The woe of these women who live in huts.[30]

Because poor folk, serfs, and slaves, not to mention the dispossessed, have been left invisible or barely visible in history, it takes time to see out and find good examples to offer to students. But examples do exist and can be found stored on websites connected to the Internet. However, there are often problems with who wrote, drew, or composed the original and usually it was not the peasants themselves but rather educated merchants and nobles who were sympathetic to their humble status and difficult lives.

Therefore, the disinherited and the downtrodden add a fourth dimension to the overall historical picture but require intensive research skills while maintaining an active suspicion that we must do with descriptions and reports by better off and educated observers in society. Worse yet, much of what was left to us and is still communicated in our own times by email and tweet may have been composed by hostile witnesses and fearful authorities. Check the sources, doubly for the downtrodden, exiled, confined, and disinherited.

d. Inclusion and Balance

A third solution to problems arising from limited pedestals is to include more stands and more varied nominees to sit or stand on the platforms and be recognized as worthy of honor.

Inclusion means widening the scope of recognition to include those marginalized, women, ethnic groups, working-class citizens, and racial groups. Expanding recognition to underprivileged and under-recognized groups and interests within a society is smart politics and good social engineering. Giving more attention to Angel Island, the site of Asian, especially Chinese, immigration, for their role in building America would go a long way to achieve better balance with Ellis Island, the site of entry for most Western and Eastern European immigration.

Recognizing outstanding representatives of marginal groups makes them feel that they are moving to the center, and enhances a sense of social cohesion. The big problem for a social order is that those who feel themselves as the central group are often reluctant to let others in, particularly those seen as unlike the founders of the "original" culture. The greater the differences between the views of the central group and "others" groups, the more likelihood of friction and a clash of interests. Extending recognition and honor to both older and newer groups would create a better balance, one that reflects the actual population shift in society, and that integrates many stories into one greater and more nuanced tale of the whole history.

Since governments are usually at the heart of deciding who does or doesn't get recognition and a marble statue, lobbying may be directed both ways for and against inclusion. The un-included and their supporters may lobby strongly for better status and a greater role while the already included may lobby against the newcomers. A possible compromise is to keep up historical traditions, inviting newcomers to build affection for earlier heroic figures, while adding representatives to the canon of heroines/heroes that please the more recent segments of the population.

This means that inclusion cuts several ways: increasing overall membership, and expanding the number of pedestals to include newer groups, newer interests, supplemented by new cultural contributions. Older groups adopt a new list of outstanding contributors to society while retaining the traditional representatives like Washington and Lincoln, who are viewed as objects of historical affection.

For instance, Mexican-Americans have achieved considerable prominence in American life and it would be quite easy, and satisfying, to recognize their Latino and indigenous heritage. Americans have rapidly and widely adopted Mexican foods and culture so why not extend this by honoring political and artistic heroes who have contributed to U.S. society? How can foods, customs, and traditions be accepted, and why accepted, much more quickly than their human practitioners?

Much the same conundrum, acceptance of foods, products, and customs, but not people, extends to global inclusion. World leaders, world culture figures, world trade all contribute people who move from one society to another, bringing new traditions and practices, new ideas and customs, from one place to another. Yet the customs and traditions may be opposed and rejected by those receiving while the foods and products are accepted and used. Inclusion and cultural exchange can be divisive when one society sees another as "foreign" and "alien," the scale of differences may challenge the center of a social order to marginalize the newcomers just as it has marginalized subcultures within its borders.

Achieving inclusion and balance is easier said than done in real life, and easier said than taught in the presentation of history. Each culture tends to hold to its own central values and views, keeping newcomer cultures and people at the periphery even when they have proven their loyalty and identification with the dominant culture.

V. RENEWAL AND REPRESENTATION

In teaching and learning history and social science, new thinking at home and in classrooms can develop from study and review of those who are assigned, overturned, and denied pedestals. We seek to understand how and why real people or literary characters are described and represented in written reports, documentation, imagery, and sound. As we reflect on meaning and message, who rates a pedestal, and who rates demotion, who should be elevated and who downgraded, becomes clearer and leads to vigorous debate and rethinking of exaltedness and villainy in history.[31]

First, the process of renewal should proceed with a sense of detachment and observation much like that advocated by Buddhist meditation. This detachment helps with the process of gaining understanding and deepening insight into history.

Second comes increasing insight into the causes and effects of human action, developing into a critical examination of the evidence and its meaning and message, if any. Causes and effects allow a deepening sense of the cycles of history, and the underlying reasons.

Third comes a growing sense of evaluation and judgment for all who have achieved life on a pedestal, as well as a consideration of the audiences who reverence the leaders, culture heroines and heroes, and beloved figures of history. Judgments permit us to create scales of value, ratings for human character and actions, ultimately leading to justice for those visible, powerful, and honored, as well as for those who are low in status, marginal, and largely invisible.

Therefore, let's review leaders, followers, culture heroines and heroes, every figure who is viewed from below as wonderful, terrific, respected, honored, and perhaps worshipped to see if they truly qualify. We need not be nasty and supercritical, but we need principles of judgment to decide who in history can still command and deserve our loyalty and faith. And we need to seek out and demand sources that give us the whole picture, the big picture, of a figure's life and accomplishments now and in historical times.

Suspicion should rule each inquiry, each investigation, without giving any privileges. No ratings allowed until a decent portion of the evidence has been collected, reviewed, and understood through at least several competing lenses. Lenses should be picture windows to several competing, or overlapping reports from outsiders and insiders, the high and the mighty, the lowly and the common, on anyone, any time and place, in the historical and social record.

The Bodhi would say that "Salvation, not destruction, assistance and mercy, not conflict and clashing forces, must rule" as the central and protective value.

Representation on pedestals should be expanded to ordinary citizens trying to help others, even to downtrodden and marginalized citizens. We should seek out the stories of those in history who are both visible and invisible.

Bodhi is a classic volunteer who assists the lives of others is the ancient Buddhist concept of a being who gives up the opportunity to achieve success, fame, riches, and ultimately nirvana, release from reality, for themselves, to continue existing to help others in their time of need.

Interestingly, maybe ironically, the Bodhi is almost always on a pedestal trying to reach and communicate with suffering humanity. The mantra of a Bodhisattva guides our thinking about the meaning of heroism and human caring for others.

Chapter 6

Bodhisattva Prayer for All Humanity

May I be a guard for those who need protection,
a guide for those on the path,
a boat, a raft, a bridge for those who wish to cross the flood.
May I be a lamp in the darkness,
a resting place for the weary,
a healing medicine for all who are sick,
a vase of plenty, a tree of miracles.
And for the boundless multitudes of living beings,
may I bring sustenance and awakening,
enduring like the earth and sky
until all beings are freed from sorrow
and all are awakened.

Shanti Deva, Indian Buddhist sage 700 AD[32]

KEY QUESTIONS TO CONSIDER, APPLY, AND EVOLVE

- What do the people we place on pedestals say about us, and past societies?
- Why do people choose to view some individuals as great while forgetting others?
- Why do nations, and empires, honor mostly aggressive men?
- Where are women leaders, or just ordinary women, raised on pedestals?
- What makes for importance in history?
- What do the social sciences have to say about race and gender in recognition?
- Are there patterns to those honored by statues? Why or why not?
- Where are statues of ordinary people?
- What do people tend to value over the course of history?
- Do any societies value women, minorities, and the downtrodden?
- Are there controversies about those honored? Why?
- Can more equality be expressed in those we honor in texts, statues, and film?

NOTES

1. *Merriam-Webster Dictionary*, s.v. "Pedestal," accessed January 20, 2021, https://www.merriam-webster.com/dictionary/pedestal..
2. Jung, C. (1971). *The Portable Jung*. New York: Viking.

3. Campbell, J. (1949). *The Hero with a Thousand Faces.* Princeton, NJ: Princeton Univ. Press.

4. Hook, S. (1943). *The Hero in History.* New York: The John Day Co.

5. Fontana, D. (1994). *The Secret Language of Symbols: A Visual Key to Symbols and Their Meanings.* San Francisco: Chronicle books.

6. Moore, R., and Gillette, D. (1990). *King, Warrior, Magician, Lover: Rediscovering the Archetypes of the Mature Masculine.* New York: HarperCollins, Inc.

7. LaCapria, K. (2 November 2016). "Snopes' Field Guide to Fake News Sites and Hoax Purveyors" Snopes.com, snopes.com. Retrieved 16 November 2016.

8. Foner, P. (2014). *Reconstruction Updated Edition: America's Unfinished Revolution, 1863–1877.* New York: Harper & Row.

9. Thucydides, History of the Peloponnesian War, 2.34–2.46. Greek text and English translation thereof available online at the Perseus Project.@ www.perseus-project.org.

10. Barton, K. (2005). "Primary sources in history: Breaking through the myths" *Phi Delta Kappan* 86, 745–753.

11. Feely, T. (2013) "Predicting students' use of evidence: An aspect of critical thinking" *Theory and Research in Education* 3, 63–72.

12. Willis, R. (Ed.) (1993). *World Mythology.* New York: Henry Holt.

13. Miles, R. (1989). *The Women's History of the World.* Salem House Publishers.

14. Gilmore, D. D. (1990). *Manhood in the Making: Cultural Concepts of Masculinity.* New Haven, CT: Yale Univ. Press.

15. Khan, S. (2004). *Psychology of the Hero Soul. Connect with Your Inner Hero.* Toronto: Diamond Mind Publishing.

16. Wolf, E. (1982, 2010). *Europe and the People Without History.* Berkeley, CA: University of California Press.

17. Durant, W. (2001). *Heroes of History: A Brief History of the World From Ancient Times to.*

18. Dundes, A., Rank, O., and Raglan, L. (1990). *In Quest of the Hero.* Princeton, NJ: Princeton Univ. Press.

19. Bolen, J. S. (1989). *Gods in Everyman.* San Francisco: Harper & Row.

20. Hadas, M. (1965). *Heroes and Gods.* New York: Harper & Row.

21. Raphael, R. (2014). *Founding Myths: Stories that Hide Our Patriotic Past.* New York: The New Press.

22. http://historysheroes.e2bn.org/heroes/suggested

23. Bentley, E. (1944). *A Century of Hero-Worship the Cult of the Superman.* Philadelphia, PA: J. B. Lippincott Co.

24. King, D. (1997). *The Commissar Vanishes: The Falsification of Photographs and Art in Stalin's Russia.* New York: Metropolitan Books.

25. Bounegru, Liliana, Gray, Jonathan, Venturini, Tommaso, and Mauri, Michele (January 8, 2018). *A Field Guide to "Fake News" and Other Information Disorders.* Amsterdam: Public Data Lab. An open access guide exploring the use of digital methods to study false viral news, political memes, trolling practices and their social life online.

26. Young, K. (2017). *Bunk: The Rise of Hoaxes, Humbug, Plagiarists, Phonies, Post-Facts, and Fake News*. Graywolf Press.

27. White, A. (March, 2019). "What schools teach about women's history leaves a lot to be desired" Smithsonian Magazine www.smithsonian.org

28. Zevin, J., and Gerwin, D. (2007). *Teaching World History as Mystery*. New York and London: Routledge.

29. Yee, J. (2005). Critical anti-racism praxis: The concept of whiteness implicated. In S. Hick, J. Fook and R. Pozzuto (Eds.), *Social Work, A Critical Turn* (pp. 87–104). Toronto: Thompson.

30. William Langland, tr. George Economou. (1996). *William Langland's Piers Plowman: The C Version: A Verse Translation*. University of Pennsylvania Press, 82.

32. Zevin, J. (2015). *Social Studies for the 21st Century*. New York and London: Routledge.

33. https://goldenageofgaia.com/2018/02/18/bodhisattva-prayer-for-humanity/

Index

bias: appearances, physical variation, 59–60; definitions, 56; differences, 59 (appearances, 61–62; belief systems, 64–65; customs, 62–63; fears, 65–66; the human condition: inferiority/superiority, 73–74; language, 53–64); identity, 58–59 (ethnocentric and narcissistic, 75–76; institutional/political partisanship/power, 74–75); inherent prejudices, 3 (likes and dislikes, 56; superiority/inferiority complex, 76); insiders/outsiders, 57–58

codes of meaning: class, 68; culture, 70–71

critical thinking: as problem solving, 4, 28; as a search for admissible evidence, 29–33; in social studies, 3

digital age: expressing historical feelings, 15–16; overwhelming resources, 12–14; real news or fake, 17

facts/evidence: age-old problems, 12, 30–32; arc of inquiry, 2; definitions, 28; idea of facts as historical evidence and law, 32–33; tales of travel: hearsay as evidence, 16–21, 33–36

gender, 69–70; race, 64–68 (Irish example, 67); zealots' patriotism/ideology, 72–73 (examples of eagle symbols in history, 72–73)

history teaching: assertions about history, 9; core principles, 51–52; teaching as historical habits of mind, 4, 39–42; teaching as "real," 5; teaching as un-privileging, 4; teaching history as "self-centered," 3; teaching with a global overview, 4–5

information overload: clouds of data, 9–10; deluge of news and views, 9; supporting evidence and corroboration, 28–29

invitations: create your own challenge, 21–22; facts and fakes, 23–24, 52, 77, 100, 128–29, 162; key questions to consider, apply, and evolve; open-mindedness, 123–27; taking new perspectives, 121–22

key questions to consider, apply, and evolve, 23–24, 52, 77, 100, 128–29, 162 lenses: agreement more likely or less likely, 118–21; appearances, 58–60; belief systems/religions, 64–65 (examining attitudes and worldviews, 123–24); customs, 62–64; definitions, 104; fear and loathing, 65–66; language differences, 63–64; lesson in perspectives, 105–11 (shared values and common loyalties, 119–21); multiple perspectives, 3, 14–15, 104–105, 114, 118–19; position and role, 111–112 (personal history, 115–16); standing in others' shoes, 113–14 (conflicts and actions, 117–18; passions and pressures, 116–17); upbringing, affiliations, ideologies, ad religions, 112–13

memory: continuity and exhaustion, 47–48; fact and invention, 48–49; people like me on a pedestal, 152–60
mythology and history: pictures and sources: Ammianus Marcellinus, view of the Huns, 60–62; Bodhisattva Prayer for all humanity, 162; bust of Pericles, famous Greek leader and orator, 135; Catherine the Great of Russia, a portrait, 140; Christopher Columbus statue vandalized, 153; Commodore Matthew Perry, USN, one photo and two Japanese artists' views compared, 106, 108–109; *Common Sense* by Thomas Paine, pamphlet over, 83–84; Empress Cixi in Royal Court, circa 1900, 89; Expedition of Lewis and Clark, 35–36; Flavius, J. *Testimonium Flavianum: a report on the life of Jesus Christ*, 41–42; Goldsworthy, A., *Tales of Ancient Rome*, 22–24; Head of Zeus in marble, 132; Homer and the story of Cyclops the Giant, 33–36; letter from King Afonso the Kongo dynasty to the King of Portugal, 110–11; Mandeville, Sir John, *Tales from Mandeville's travels*, 17–23; Map of the Sea of Marmara, home of Troy and many stories, 34–35; Nikolai Lenin giving a revolutionary speech, with photo doctored later to erase people, 148; Peasants Revolt in Germany, 158; proposed statue of Suffragettes for Central Park, NY, 122; San Lorenzo Colossal Olmec Head, 136–38; She-Wolf Mother of twin founders of Rome, Romulus and Remus, 79–80; Statue of Pharaoh Menkaura and Queen Khamerenebty, 128; Weatherford, J., *Tales of Genghis Khan*, 22–24

pedestals: 9/11 responders as ordinary heroes, heroines, 154–55; becoming visible, 144 (celebrated and suppressed, 146–49; central and marginal, 149–51; repressed and reclaimed, 150–52; visible and invisible, 145); Christopher Columbus and others attacked, 152–54; definitions, 131–32; inclusion and balance, 159–60; leaders and followers, 138–39; lifestyles and charisma, 141–42; meaning and message of pedestals, 132–38; moral symbols and entertainment values, 143–44; people like me on a pedestal: recognition and representation, 152–60 (compliance and complaint, 152–54; downtrodden and disinherited, 156–59; inclusion and balance, 159–60; ordinary heroines and heroes, 154–56); reflected identity, 139–41; renewal and representation, 160–62
pictures and photos. *See under* mythology and history

rules for historical detectives: organizing investigations, 14; playing time and space traveler, 125–26; quick and easy rules, 13; renewal and representation, 160–62; suspending loyalties, 124–25

social studies: applying lenses to history from the many media we have, 126–28; cell phones to net streams, 8; C3 Framework of NCSS, 3; modern technology and teaching, 5–7; the new social studies of the 1960s and 1970s, 2–3

sources, primary and secondary: primary sources as original, 39–41; secondary sources as summaries, 42–44; tertiary sources as overviews of other sources, 44–51

story: bringing history to literature and literature to history, 35–38; developing multiple narratives, 96–97 (human emotions and limitations, 97–98; storytelling: originals and embellishments, 98–99); genre: real and imagined, 86–87 (characters, 90–91; plot and action, 88–90; structure and flow, 87–88); overall judgments of stories and histories and herstories, 91–92; storytelling across genres, 100; straightforward to symbolic stories, 92–93 (believability and agenda, 93–95; the moral of the story, 95–96); truth as story, 33–36 (as history/social science, 85–86; as journal, 81–84; as literature, 81; as testimony, 84–85)

suspicion: of bias, of stories, of interpretations, of views, and of pedestals, 11; of facts, 10, 11; of sources, 8, 12, 14–16 (and provenance, 30–41); of truth as inference, 36–38

understanding historical context: context: time and place, memory continuity and loss, 45–52; grasping life and gaining insight, 15

About the Author

Jack Zevin is recently emeritus from Queens College/City University of New York) having taught there for just about fifty years, leaving a wealth of students who have joined the ranks of teachers of history and the social sciences. He is steady and productive author of books about teaching history and social science, as well as teaching creatively and with verve. Jack has authored a standard methods book in the field, *Social Studies for the 21st Century*, currently heading toward its fifth edition. Jack has also received numerous teaching awards and grants over the years, including best teacher at QC, Global award from the NCSS, and The President's award from the New York ATSS/UFT social studies organization. He has co-authored books on geography education, and two volumes on teaching history as mystery with a colleague, David Gerwin. Jack has a longstanding love of history, and the social sciences, mixed with ecology and many sciences, as well as the humanities. Jack loves wandering through history, art, music, and literature inviting all of his students and you, his readers to join in a walkabout through unfamiliar territories.

Overall, Jack has contributed simulations and role-plays for decades in social studies with the aim of building creative and gifted instruction across subjects for a variety of classrooms.

www.ingramcontent.com/pod-product-compliance
Lightning Source LLC
Chambersburg PA
CBHW052048300426
44117CB00012B/2034